The Quilt Room

That Patchwork Place®

Pam Lintott and Rosemary Miller

DEDICATION

This book is dedicated to all who possess the love of quiltmaking. They share a language without barriers, making it possible for quiltmakers all over the world to communicate.

ACKNOWLEDGMENTS

Thanks go to:
our mothers, Rose and Audrey,
for their skill in teaching us the basics of sewing—may we all continue to teach the next generation; our husbands and children for their continuing support; our loyal customers.

Credits

Editor-in-Chief . . . . Barbara Weiland
Technical Editor . . . . Ursula Reikes
Managing Editor . . . . Greg Sharp
Copy Editor . . . . Liz McGehee
Proofreader . . . . Leslie Phillips
Design Director . . . . Judy Petry
Text and Cover Designer . . . . Kay Green
Design Assistant . . . . Shean Bemis
Illustrator . . . . Brian Metz
Illustration Assistant . . . . Lisa McKenney
Cover Art Illustrator . . . . Thomas Boatman
Photographer (unless otherwise noted) . . . . Brent Kane

The Quilt Room
©1995 by Pam Lintott and Rosemary Miller

That Patchwork Place Inc.
PO Box 118
Bothell, WA 98041-0118
USA

Printed in Hong Kong
00 99 98 97 96 95   6 5 4 3 2 1

Library of Congress Cataloging-in-Publication Data
Lintott, Pam.
    The quilt room / Pam Lintott and Rosemary Miller
        p.   cm.
    ISBN 1-56477-097-4
    1. Patchwork—Patterns. 2. Appliqué—Patterns. I. Miller, Rosemary. II. Title.
TT835.L5662 1995
746.46—dc20   95-13637
                                        CIP

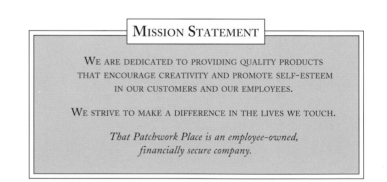

MISSION STATEMENT

WE ARE DEDICATED TO PROVIDING QUALITY PRODUCTS THAT ENCOURAGE CREATIVITY AND PROMOTE SELF-ESTEEM IN OUR CUSTOMERS AND OUR EMPLOYEES.

WE STRIVE TO MAKE A DIFFERENCE IN THE LIVES WE TOUCH.

That Patchwork Place is an employee-owned, financially secure company.

Contents

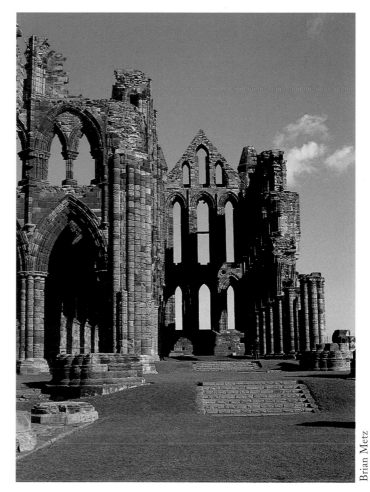

Brian Metz

Whitby Abbey

Welcome to England

Sheep being herded up West Street in Dorking at the turn of the century. Reprinted with permission from the Dorking and District Museum.

DORKING— AN OLD ENGLISH TOWN

Dorking is fifteen miles from London and thirty miles from the coast. In the days when travel was really horse power and an overnight stop for such a journey was necessary to rest the horses, Dorking was ideally situated. It became a market town with many inns and public houses.

One of these inns, the Wheatsheaf Inn, where The Quilt Room first opened, dates back to 1450. The Wheatsheaf Inn became famous for offering the dubious entertainment of cockfighting, and the circular cockfighting pit is still there today, deep underground, beneath the shop. Sandstone lies underneath the town, and this was exploited on a grand scale, with caves and tunnels linking

Pump Corner in Dorking, about 1850, showing the high pavement that still exists today. Reprinted with permission from the Dorking and District Museum.

The Quilt Room on West Street in Dorking as it exists today.

numerous areas of the town underground. These caves and tunnels attracted smugglers, and for a while, Dorking had a reputation as a smugglers' town. At one time, tunnels linked the Wheatsheaf Inn to other inns and even the church! It is not surprising that tales of it being haunted abound.

In 1750, the Wheatsheaf Inn proprietor, who was famous for rearing hogs, had one of the largest pigs ever seen in England. This grand specimen broke its leg and had to be killed, but it was stuffed and became a showpiece, attracting visitors for miles around. Had it lived to be fatted, it might have tipped the scales at 2,800 pounds!

Dorking was also the home of William Mullins, a shoemaker, who in 1620 sailed on the Mayflower to America. His impressive house still stands opposite The Quilt Room on West Street and now houses four antique shops. It is said to be the only existing English home that once belonged to a Pilgrim Father.

Dorking is surrounded on all sides by hills, which form part of the North Downs, and it is designated an Area of Natural Beauty.

HISTORY OF THE QUILT ROOM

In 1980, my husband, Nick, and I (Pam) converted the old Wheatsheaf Inn into a bookshop. A year later, we turned one of the first-floor rooms that had a beam ceiling into The Quilt Room. The beams created a splendid display area for the brightly coloured quilts, transforming the room into a magical Aladdin's Cave. Yes, it started as a hobby—haven't you heard that before?—but soon became a business that occupied my time seven days a week and more.

By 1988, The Quilt Room had become too small, and we moved it to a new location in the centre of the antique district. It stands out brightly there amongst the oak dressers and mahogany tables of its neighbours. When we first moved in, we couldn't believe the amount of space we had, but in recent years, we are all quite sure that the shop has shrunk! Our 1500 bolts of fabric and 500 book titles couldn't have anything to do with it!

In 1993, we moved our mail-order department to its own premises on the edge of town. It is only half a mile

from the shop but it borders onto farmland, and we have had to get used to deer and squirrels knocking over our milk bottles and cows wandering across our car park. We now have a lot more space, but we do expect that building to start shrinking soon!

ABOUT THE AUTHORS

Pam and Rosemary

Pam's interest in quilts began back in 1970 when she was living in America and saw other forms of patchwork from around the world. She spent three years in America and then, complete with backpacks, she and her husband, Nick, set out for Australia, taking a route not so easily travelled today, via Iran and Afghanistan. They travelled slowly, taking in the culture of each individual country, and spent a year touring Australia before returning to England. Still with itchy feet, they bought a yacht and lived on it for two years in the Mediterranean. (Pam sewed endless hexagons in the sunshine!) The arrival of their first child, Nicola, made them decide to return to England to put down roots, and their sons, Robert and Michael, followed in quick succession. When Pam started The Quilt Room in 1981, her children were still very small. Michael, who was born in 1982, slept in an antique crib in the shop, and when not asleep, was passed from customer to customer while fabric was chosen and cut. He doesn't seem to have suffered any ill effects!

Rosemary arrived on the scene in 1983 and from there they have gone from strength to strength. When a partnership works well, daunting tasks suddenly seem no more than minor problems that are fun to solve together. Sharing the load seems to make the burden not just half as light but almost weightless.

Rosemary first learned the basics of needlework from her mother, and sewing has always been part of her life. After completing school, she went on to learn catering and was a successful free-lance cook before and during the early part of her marriage. After the arrival of her two children, Patrick and Katrina, she spent the next few years caring for them and looking after her husband, David. She sewed only occasionally. And then one day, a friend showed her a beautiful Log Cabin quilt. That was it—she was hooked. It inspired her to start making her own, which was the beginning of an enthralling hobby—and subsequently a thriving business! Rosemary's love of fabric, together with the element of mathematical calculations, make quilting for her a most challenging and creative hobby.

PikeRiver Films Limited

MEET THE REST OF THE TEAM

We expanded our mail-order department in 1993 when Pat Keating and Hilary Longhurst joined us. Before that, we could say that we had all been together for more than ten years.

Sharon Chambers manages the shop and she still has her Texan accent even though she has been here for more than twenty-five years. She teaches our beginners and guides them through to the intermediate level. After twelve weeks with Sharon, they are always hooked.

We persuaded Pam Anstey to move from the shop to run the mail-order department, which she does extremely efficiently, but she misses the customers so much, we have to let her back into the shop on a Saturday! She also teaches many of the quick rotary-cutting and machine-quilting classes. The daunting task of quilting The Woman's Hour Quilt truly put her talents to the test, but she passed with flying colours.

Joan Taylor has been with us right from the beginning, and although she left us to go travelling with her husband for a few years, we were delighted when she rejoined us. She can remember when we actually kept a sewing machine in the shop and had time during the day to sit and sew. The remainder of the team—Tina Lamborn, Margaret Hughes, Jean Davidson, and Pat Lander—are also great quiltmakers and teach various classes.

Teaching has always been high on the list of priorities at The Quilt Room. From September to April, we

WORKSHOPS

Workshop in progress:
Barbara Barker teaches intricate piecing.

PikeRiver Films Limited

hold workshops virtually every day of the week. The workshops are always full and, more importantly, always fun. In addition to workshops given by The Quilt Room staff, we arrange for tutors to come from all over the country to teach and have the added pleasure of their company when they stay overnight. We consider ourselves very lucky to have made such good friends in this way. Some of our regular tutors include Deirdre Amsden, Susan Denton, Rita Humphry, Lynne Edwards, Irene MacWilliam, and Pauline Burbidge, all of whom have that enviable combination of great talent plus the capability of inspiring and teaching others.

PikeRiver Films Limited

Top row (left to right):
Tina, Hilary, Rosemary, Pam Lintott, Sharon, Pat Landers;
Bottom row (left to right):
Jean, Pam Anstey, Margaret, Joan, Pat Keating.

THE WOMAN'S HOUR QUILT

When the first telephone call came from the BBC (British Broadcasting Corporation) asking for our assistance in this project, we little dreamed that we would be involved in creating a quilt with such historic significance. The long-running programme, "Woman's Hour" on Radio 4, wanted to commemorate the seventy-fifth anniversary of the Suffragette Movement and invited their listeners to sew a block representing some aspect of women's achievements since gaining the right to vote. The quilt is a powerful statement of those achievements and hung impressively in the House of Commons as part of an exhibition. It is now touring the country, and it will eventually be housed at the Victoria and Albert Museum in London.

A whole range of techniques is represented in this quilt—piecing, appliqué, reverse appliqué, painting, and dyeing. There is hand and machine quilting, embroidery, and three-dimensional embellishments. The blocks are incredibly varied. Some depict the professions that women have entered, others honour individual women for their contribution, and others depict ideas in a more abstract way. A great deal of imagination and work went into the blocks, making the task of choosing which ones to use that much harder.

We spent an incredibly difficult day with Helen Galley and Jenny Murray of the BBC selecting the blocks. Then began the mammoth task of assembling the quilt. The 10" blocks ranged from about 8" to 11", necessitating some thoughtful additions or rather more difficult subtractions. Without Sharon Chambers and Pam Anstey, the quilt would never have been finished in time. The amount of work they put in was certainly beyond the call of duty! We did all the work in our workroom, and shop customers were able to view it in progress. The suffragette colours of purple and green were chosen for the sashing and borders, and on the lower border are embroidered the names of all the women politicians in Parliament at that time. This was certainly a project in which we were very happy and proud to be involved.

The Woman's Hour Quilt, 1993, England. Blocks for this quilt were submitted by listeners to the BBC Woman's Hour to celebrate seventy-five years of women's suffrage. The quilt was completed by the staff at The Quilt Room, Dorking. (Photo courtesy of the British Broadcasting Corporation)

Fabric Selection

To be confronted by bolts and bolts of fabric often confuses even the most experienced quiltmaker. Don't panic. Look around and pick out one fabric that you really like. Try to find one that includes a number of the colours you want in your quilt or one that contains the basic colour you had in mind. Also keep in mind the effect that colours have on the viewer. Red, orange, and yellow are considered warm colours, and green, blue, and purple are considered cool colours. When warm and cool colours are combined in a quilt, the warm colours will come forward and be dominant, while the cool colours will recede. When choosing the fabrics to accompany your first choice, always remember these three important points: colour, value, and scale.

COLOUR

A little knowledge of colour and its effects can be very useful, but do not let too much theory subdue your own natural flair and ability. The twelve basic colours are usually displayed in a circle or wheel. They are made up of three groups of colours.

Primary colours—red, yellow, and blue—are pure colours and cannot be obtained by mixing. They form the points of an equilateral triangle on the colour wheel.

Secondary colours are made by mixing equal proportions of two adjacent primary colours.

red + yellow = orange
yellow + blue = green
red + blue = purple

Intermediate colours are made by mixing adjacent primary and secondary colours.

yellow + orange = yellow-orange
red + orange = red-orange
red + purple = red-purple
blue + purple = blue-purple
blue + green = blue-green
yellow + green = yellow-green

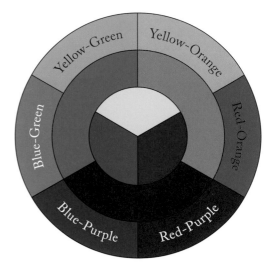

The addition of white, black, and grey further alters the colour to produce tints, shades, and tones.

Tints are made by adding white.

Shades are made by adding black.

Tones are made by adding grey to produce a dulled hue—one that is less intense.

There are three basic colour schemes based on the colour wheel. If you are a bit uncomfortable selecting fabrics for a quilt, try choosing fabrics in one of the following colour schemes.

Monochromatic colour schemes are made with tints, shades, and tones of one colour.

Complementary colour schemes are made with colours that are opposite each other on the colour wheel.

Analogous colour schemes are made with colours that are next to each other on the colour wheel.

VALUE

Value is the degree of lightness or darkness in a colour. Value is the most important consideration when choosing fabrics—even more so than colour. A well-balanced quilt needs the contrast between light, medium, and dark. Value is relative, so it is not until you put your fabrics together that the right balance can be judged. Using a reducing glass or looking through the wrong end of binoculars can help in checking relative values, but standing back from your fabrics and squinting is also effective!

SCALE

Scale refers to the size of the pattern or motif on a printed fabric. Small prints have long been popular with quiltmakers, although the designers of antique quilts seem to have been far more adventurous, sometimes using quite outrageous fabrics to great effect. Quiltmakers are again exploring the possibilities of large-scale prints, producing exciting combinations and adding new dimensions to our quilts.

Your fabric choices should combine to produce a balance that is harmonious but not too predictable. Try a mixture of solids, large and small prints, geometric designs, plaids, and stripes. It may be that once all your fabrics are chosen, you decide to discard your very first choice. That's fine—it's served its purpose and sent you in the right direction. Don't forget to check your fabric selection from a distance as well as close up.

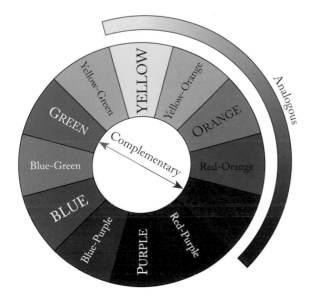

Fabric Facts

All cotton fabric is made up of two woven threads. The lengthwise thread is called the warp and is taut with little or no give. The crosswise thread that runs from selvage to selvage is called the weft and has just a little give. Selvages are the edges of the fabric and these should be removed before using. A cut made diagonally across the warp and the weft is made "on the bias." Fabric stretches on the bias; therefore, when you are cutting fabric for patchwork, care should be taken to place templates on the straight of grain, that is, parallel to the lengthwise or crosswise threads.

Fabric should be washed before it is used. This will remove all sizing and loose dye and will shrink the fabric before it is sewn. Unfold all fabric. Separate the darks and lights and wash in tepid water either by hand or in the machine. It is not necessary to use soap powder, but if you do, use a mild one. If you prefer to work with new, unwashed fabrics, they should be tested for colourfastness; cut a small square from each fabric and wash as described above. All fabric requirements in this book are based on 44"-wide fabric and allow for 5% shrinkage.

To prevent fabric from fraying and tangling while being washed, snip a small triangle off all four corners. This will also tell you which fabrics have been washed once they are placed on your shelves.

To stop colours from bleeding, add a ¼ cup of salt to the last rinse water and let the fabric soak for 15 minutes. Another method is to soak the fabric in a solution of 3 parts cold water to 1 part white vinegar. If the fabric still bleeds, do not use it or make sure that the finished quilt is dry-cleaned. Remember, though, that if your quilt accidentally gets wet, it could bleed.

Big Ben

Claudia L'Heureux

Fabric Shopping Tip

If you find yourself in a quilt shop and are tempted to buy some fabric without any particular design in mind, buy a half yard of fabrics that just look good, 1 yard of ones you can't live without, 2 yards of ones that are a good background, 2½ yards of border fabrics, and 5 yards of backing fabrics. Bear in mind that between 9 and 10 yards are needed for a double quilt, 6 yards for a single, and 2 or 3 yards for a cot or crib quilt. Remember that you may not be able to purchase the fabric again and think of the wonderful scrap quilts you can make with any leftovers.

The Projects

The quilts we selected for this book range from the very traditional to the more contemporary and cover a variety of themes from florals to sheep. Some are quick and easy to piece, while a few require a little more time.

The four floral samplers represent the four seasons which, in England, are quite varied. "An Englishman's home is his castle" is a well-known expression but it is in their gardens that the English reign supreme. Quilters especially seem to love gardening, and you can be sure that when the sun is shining, many of our customers put down their quilting and take up their gardening tools. In a way, you can see the similarity in patchwork and in the garden—it is the variety of colour and texture that creates the overall effect. The floral samplers are made entirely from triangles and squares, cut with the rotary cutter, machine pieced, and machine quilted. Since the quilts require a variety of scraps, we suggest cutting the half-square triangles as described on pages 79–80.

When deciding on which quilts to include, it became apparent that we had all made our fair share of scrap quilts. One suggestion about why we like scrap quilts so much is that it gives us the best excuse possible for rummaging through our fabrics—and that could well be the truth.

Some quilters love handwork. Whether it's covering little pieces of paper with fabric for the Star Turn quilt or doing broderie perse for the Cream on Cream quilt, there is something very peaceful about the time spent with needle and fabric in hand.

Before you start the projects in this book, refer to the "Basic Techniques," beginning on page 78. Many general instructions and techniques not covered in the individual projects are presented there. It's always a good idea to review these instructions.

Spring Flowers

By Pam Lintott & Rosemary Miller

Spring Flowers by Pam Lintott and Rosemary Miller, 1994, Dorking, England, 56" x 56".
Machine pieced and machine quilted.

S*pring in England is one of our favourite times. Primroses cover the banks of the country lanes, and the tulips and daffodils brighten up the gardens and parks. This quilt is made from scraps of yellows, oranges, and reds; the more scraps you have, the brighter the quilt. Three different flower blocks are used for the centre—Daffodil, Tulip, and Primrose—and a modified version of the Tulip block is used for the pieced border. As so many different fabrics were used, the fabric quantities are only a guide.*

Materials: 44"-wide fabric

Purchase an assortment of fabrics to total the amounts given below.

¾ yd. total assorted red scraps

¼ yd. total assorted orange scraps

⅞ yd. total assorted yellow scraps

½ yd. total assorted green scraps

2⅜ yds. cream background
(includes sashing and borders)

½ yd. red for binding

3½ yds. backing

Cutting

All measurements include ¼"-wide seam allowances.

From the assorted red scraps, cut:
   52 squares, each 2½" x 2½"
   51 squares, each 2⅞" x 2⅞"; cut squares once diagonally to yield 102 half-square triangles

From the assorted orange scraps, cut:
   15 squares, each 2½" x 2½"
   9 squares, each 2⅞" x 2⅞"; cut squares once diagonally to yield 18 half-square triangles

From the assorted yellow scraps, cut:
   66 squares, each 2½" x 2½"
   73 squares, each 2⅞" x 2⅞"; cut squares once diagonally to yield 146 half-square triangles

From the assorted green scraps, cut:
   8 squares, each 4½" x 4½"
   20 squares, each 2½" x 2½", for leaves and cornerstones and corner squares
   26 squares, each 2⅞" x 2⅞"; cut squares once diagonally to yield 52 half-square triangles

From the cream fabric, cut:
   7 strips, each 2⅞" x 42"; crosscut into 91 squares, each 2⅞" x 2⅞"; cut squares once diagonally to yield 182 half-square triangles
   1 piece, 42" x 58"; cut 10 strips, each 2½" x 58", from the lengthwise grain of the fabric

From the remainder of the cream fabric (approximately 18" x 58"), cut:
   14 strips, each 2½" x 18"; crosscut into 98 squares, each 2½" x 2½"
   5 strips, each 2⅞" x 18"; crosscut into 25 squares, each 2⅞" x 2⅞"; cut squares once diagonally to yield 50 half-square triangles

From the red fabric, cut:
   6 strips, each 2½" x 42", for binding

Tip

Don't forget that the wrong side of the fabric can often be used to obtain a different shade of green for the stalks and leaves of flowers.

Directions

1. Following the block diagrams below, arrange the assorted squares and half-square triangles. Join the half-square triangles to make pieced squares. Join the squares and pieced squares in horizontal rows; press the seams in opposite directions from row to row. Join the rows to complete the blocks. Make 3 Daffodil blocks, 3 Tulip blocks, and 3 Primrose blocks.

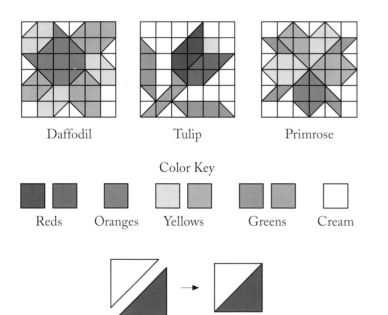

Daffodil   Tulip   Primrose

Color Key

Reds   Oranges   Yellows   Greens   Cream

2. Using 6 of the 2½" x 58" cream strips, cut:
   4 strips, each 2½" x 40½", for inner borders
   12 strips, each 2½" x 12½", for sashing.
   Reserve the remaining 4 strips for the outer border.

3. Assemble the blocks in 3 horizontal rows of 3 blocks each, adding cream sashing strips between the blocks. Press the seams towards the sashing strips.

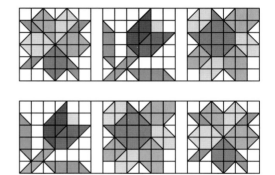

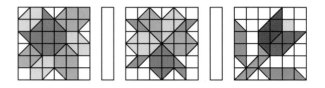

4. Join 3 cream sashing strips and 2 green cornerstones to make 1 sashing row. Make 2 rows.

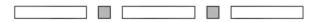

5. Sew the sashing rows between the rows of blocks. Refer to the colour photo on page 14. Press the seams towards the sashing rows.

6. Sew 2 of the 2½" x 40½" inner border cream strips to opposite sides of the quilt top. Sew a 2½" green square to opposite ends of each of the remaining 2½" x 40½" cream strips; stitch to the top and bottom edges.

7. Join squares and half-square triangles to make 40 Tulip border blocks.

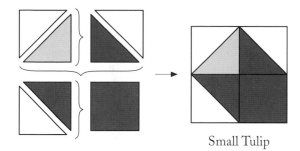

Small Tulip

8. Using the 4½" green squares and the 2½" cream squares, make 8 Square within a Square blocks. Mark a diagonal line on the wrong side of the small cream squares. Place 2 cream squares on opposite corners of the large green square, right sides together. Sew on the marked diagonal line. Trim the excess fabric about ¼" from the seam; finger-press the triangle to the corner. Repeat with 2 cream squares on the remaining corners.

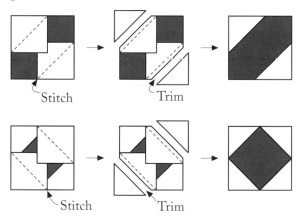

Stitch   Trim

Stitch   Trim

9. Join 10 Tulip blocks and 1 Square within a Square block to make each of the side borders.

Make 2

10. Join 10 Tulip blocks and 3 Square within a Square blocks to make each of the top and bottom borders.

Make 2

11. Sew the side border strips to the quilt first, then add the top and bottom border strips.

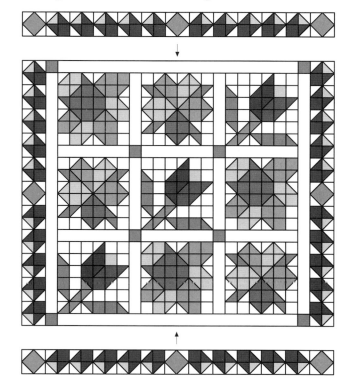

12. Following directions on pages 83–84 for straight-cut borders, measure, cut, and sew the outer borders to the quilt.

13. Layer the quilt with batting and backing; baste. Quilt as desired and bind the edges. We quilted in-the-ditch around the petals of each flower and in a diagonal grid on the sashing and inner and outer borders.

14. Sign and date your quilt.

Herbaceous Border

By Pam Lintott & Rosemary Miller

Herbaceous Border by Pam Lintott and Rosemary Miller, 1994, Dorking, England, 64" x 84".
Machine pieced. Beautifully machine quilted by Barbara Barber, who gallantly
came to our rescue when we were trying to meet our deadlines.

The herbaceous border is an essential feature of the English country garden. In midsummer, it is a blaze of purples, blues, mauves, pinks, and reds. We chose Liberty of London™ Tana™ Lawn prints for this quilt since their colours match our herbaceous borders perfectly. The quilt is made up of four different blocks, three of each design. The blocks are pieced together with a Garden Maze sashing.

Materials: 44"-wide fabric

Note: If you wish to use Liberty Tana Lawn prints, you will need to purchase more fabric since it is only 36" wide.

2 yds. total assorted prints

⅝ yd. total assorted green scraps

1¾ yds. cream for background

2⅜ yds. print for Garden Maze sashing and binding

1⅝ yds. solid pink for Garden Maze sashing

4 yds. backing

Claudia L'Heureux

Anne Hathaway's Cottage

Cutting

Cut strips across the width of the fabric.
All measurements include ¼"-wide seam allowances.

From the assorted prints, cut:

approximately 207 squares, each 2½" x 2½" (This number will vary, depending on how many different fabrics you have and in which flower you are using them.)

approximately 158 squares, each 2⅞" x 2⅞"; cut squares once diagonally to yield 316 half-square triangles (Again, this number will vary.)

From the assorted green scraps, cut:

27 squares, each 2½" x 2½"

48 squares, each 2⅞" x 2⅞"; cut squares once diagonally to yield 96 half-square triangles

From the cream fabric, cut:

14 strips, each 2½" x 42"; crosscut into 219 squares, each 2½" x 2½"

8 strips, each 2⅞" x 42"; crosscut into 110 squares, each 2⅞" x 2⅞"; cut squares once diagonally to yield 220 half-square triangles

From the print fabric, cut:

16 strips, each 3" x 42" for Garden Maze sashing

3 strips, each 4¼" x 42"; crosscut into 20 squares, each 4¼" x 4¼"

8 strips, each 2½" x 42", for binding

From the solid pink fabric, cut:

32 strips, each 1¼" x 42", for Garden Maze sashing

20 of Template A

40 of Template B

Directions

1. Following the block diagrams below, arrange the squares and half-square triangles. Join the half-square triangles to make pieced squares. Join the squares and pieced squares in horizontal rows; press the seams in opposite directions from row to row. Join the rows to complete the blocks. Make 3 Carnation blocks, 3 Iris blocks, 3 Aster blocks, and 3 Peony blocks.

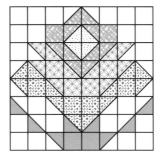
Carnation

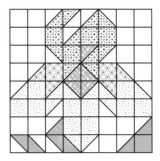
Iris

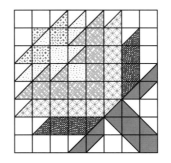
Peony

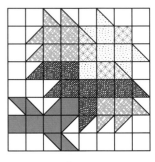
Aster

Color Key

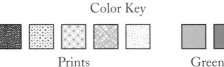

Prints   Greens

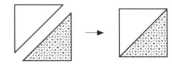

2. Join the 1¼"-wide solid pink strips and 3"-wide print strips to make 16 strip units for the Garden Maze sashing. Press the seams towards the solid pink fabric. Cut the strip units into a total of 31 segments, each 16½" long.

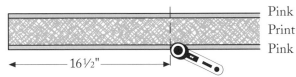

Pink
Print
Pink

16½"

3. Assemble the blocks in 4 horizontal rows of 3 blocks each, adding pieced sashing strips between the blocks and at either end. Press the seams towards the sashing strips.

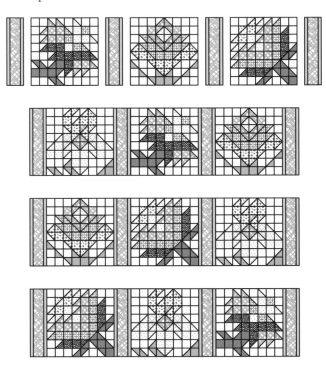

4. Cut the 4¼" print squares twice diagonally to yield 80 quarter-square triangles. Following the directions on page 80, nub the points of the triangles. Sew the short side of 2 triangles to opposite sides of solid pink piece B. Press the seams towards piece B.

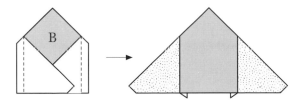

5. Join 2 units made in step 4 and a solid pink piece A to make a pieced cornerstone. Press the seams towards piece A.

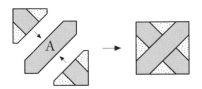

6. Join 3 pieced sashing strips and 4 pieced cornerstones to make a sashing row. Make a total of 5 rows.

7. Sew the sashing rows between the rows of blocks and at the top and bottom edges. Refer to the colour photo on page 18. Press the seams towards the sashing rows.

8. Layer the quilt with batting and backing; baste. Quilt as desired and bind the edges. Our quilt was intricately machine quilted, using different quilting patterns on the flowers and stippling on the Garden Maze sashing.

9. Sign and date your quilt.

Strawberries in Raspberry Cream

Nothing beats a combination of strawberries, tennis at Wimbledon, and English sunshine.

1 lb. strawberries
icing (confectioners') sugar for dusting
juice of ½ orange

Hull and cut the strawberries in half, place them in a glass bowl, dust with confectioners' sugar, and sprinkle with the orange juice; cover and leave in a cool place.

½ lb. raspberries
4 Tablespoons icing (confectioners') sugar
½ pint double (whipping) cream

Rub the raspberries through a nylon sieve. Work the icing sugar into this purée a little at a time. Lightly whip the cream and carefully fold in the sweetened purée. Mix thoroughly. Spoon over the strawberries and chill.

Autumn Leaves

By Pam Lintott & Rosemary Miller

*Autumn Leaves by Pam Lintott and Rosemary Miller, 1994, Dorking, England, 53¼" x 53¼".
Machine pieced. Machine quilted by Barbara Barber.*

A collection of Roberta Horton plaids was combined with a navy blue background to create this autumn quilt. We used a traditional block but gave it a slightly different look by rotating the blocks and separating them with a narrow sashing strip. The pieced striped border sets off the design nicely.

Materials: 44"-wide fabric

¼ yd. each of 12 autumn plaids

2¼ yds. navy blue

¼ yd. solid gold

½ yd. binding

3⅜ yds. backing

Cutting

Cut strips across the width of the fabric.
All measurements include ¼"-wide seam allowances.

From each of the 12 autumn plaids, cut:
1 strip, 1½" x 42", for middle pieced border
1 strip, 2⅞" x 42"; crosscut into 9 squares, each 2⅞" x 2⅞"; cut squares once diagonally to yield 18 half-square triangles for a total of 216 half–square triangles. From the remainder of the 2⅞"-wide strip, cut 3 squares, each 2½" x 2½" for a total of 36 squares.

Note: Each 2⅞" strip will yield enough squares to make 3 autumn leaves. You need a total of 36 leaves.

From the navy blue fabric, cut:
11 strips, each 2⅞" x 42"; crosscut into 144 squares, each 2⅞" x 2⅞"; cut squares once diagonally to yield 288 half-square triangles
3 strips, each 2½" x 42"; crosscut into 36 squares, each 2½" x 2½"
9 strips, each 1¼" x 42" for sashing; crosscut 5 strips into 30 segments, each 1¼" x 6½". Reserve the remaining strips for horizontal sashing.
5 strips, each 2½" x 42", for inner border
6 strips, each 2½" x 42", for outer border

From the solid gold fabric, cut:
5 strips, each 1" x 42", for leaf stems
1 strip, 1½" x 42", for middle pieced border

From the binding fabric, cut:
6 strips, each 2½" x 42"

Directions

1. Chain piece 216 navy blue and 216 plaid half-square triangles together to make pieced squares. Refer to page 81 for chain-piecing directions.

2. To make the stems, sew 36 navy blue half-square triangles to one side of the 1"-wide gold strips, leaving approximately 1" between the triangles to allow for squaring up the squares. Finger-press the triangles open.

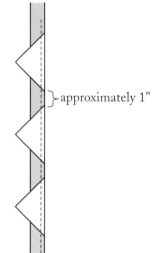

approximately 1"

3. Sew the remaining 36 navy blue half-square triangles to the other side of the gold strip, matching the tips of the triangles as shown. Press the triangles open and cut between the squares.

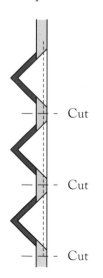

— Cut

— Cut

— Cut

4. Use a Bias Square® ruler to square up the corners of the stem units. Place the diagonal line of the Bias Square ruler on the centre of the stem and trim the first two sides of the square. Turn the unit around. With the diagonal line of the Bias Square centred on the stem, align the 2½" mark on the ruler with the edges of the square and trim the remaining 2 sides.

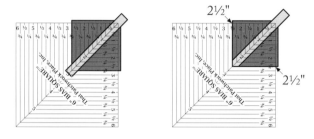

5. Following the block diagram below, arrange the squares, pieced squares, and stem unit. Be sure to use matching fabrics in each leaf block. Join the squares and pieced squares in horizontal rows; press the seams in opposite directions from row to row. Join the rows to complete the blocks. Make 36 Leaf blocks, chain piecing wherever possible.

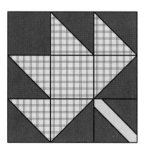

Autumn Leaves

6. Assemble the blocks in 6 horizontal rows of 6 blocks each, adding short navy blue sashing strips between the blocks. Rotate the Leaf blocks as necessary to form the pattern; refer to the color photo on page 22. Press the seams towards the sashing strips.

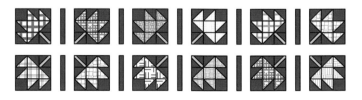

7. Measure the length of the horizontal rows of blocks and trim the remaining 1¼"-wide navy blue sashing strips to that length. Sew the sashing strips between the rows of blocks. Refer to the colour photo on page 22.

Measure

8. Following directions on pages 83–84 for straight-cut borders, measure, cut, and sew the inner navy blue border strips to the quilt.

9. To make the middle pieced border, join the 12 plaid 1½"-wide strips and 1 solid gold 1½"-wide strip to make a strip unit. Press the seams to one side. Cut the strip unit into segments, each 3"-wide.

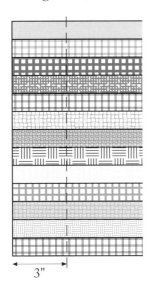

3"

10. Join the pieced segments end to end to make one long continuous strip. Following directions on pages 83–84 for straight-cut borders, measure, cut, and sew the pieced border strips to the sides first, then to the top and bottom edges of the quilt.

11. Measure, cut, and sew the outer navy blue border strips to the quilt in the same manner as the inner border.

12. Layer the quilt with batting and backing; baste. Quilt as desired and bind the edges. We machine quilted our quilt, using a variety of coloured threads.

13. Sign and date your quilt.

Elderflower Drink

20 elderflower heads
2 slices of lemon
2½ oz. citric acid
8 cups granulated sugar
1 quart boiling water

Put the elderflowers, lemon slices, citric acid, and sugar in a large bowl and add the boiling water; stir until the sugar has dissolved. Cover and leave in a cool place for 5 to 7 days, giving it a stir morning and evening. Strain into bottles and keep in the fridge. Dilute to taste with either water or lemonade.

Winter Pansies

By Pam Lintott & Rosemary Miller

Winter Pansies by Pam Lintott and Rosemary Miller, 1994, Dorking, England, 48" x 48".
Machine pieced and machine quilted.

This quilt is made from nine blocks, using different scraps of fabric for each block. We used about twelve different plain fabrics in pinks, blues, and purples. The black background in the blocks and the black sashing work together to create the illusion that the pansies are floating. A sawtooth border uses up the remaining triangles from the blocks. If you prefer a soft, delicate effect, try small prints and a cream background.

Materials: 44"-wide fabric

The following fabric quantities are based on using 4 different purples, blues, and pinks.

¼ yd. each of 12 different fabrics for pansies

¼ yd. yellow for pansy eyes

2⅝ yds. black for background, sashing, borders, and binding

3⅛ yds. backing

Cutting

All measurements include ¼"-wide seam allowances.

From each of the 12 pansy fabrics, cut:

1 strip, 2⅞" x 42"; crosscut into 13 squares, each 2⅞" x 2⅞"; cut squares once diagonally to yield 26 half-square triangles, for a total of 312 half-square triangles. You will only use 308.

1 strip, 2½" x 21"; crosscut into 8 squares, each 2½" x 2½", for a total of 72 squares.

From the yellow fabric, cut:

2 strips, each 2⅞" x 42"; crosscut into 18 squares, each 2⅞" x 2⅞"; cut squares once diagonally to yield 36 half-square triangles

From the black fabric, cut 1 piece of fabric, 42" x 46".
Then cut the following strips from the lengthwise grain:

6 strips, each 2½" x 46", for sashing and borders

6 strips, each 2⅞" x 46"; crosscut into 90 squares, each 2⅞" x 2⅞"; cut squares once diagonally to yield 180 half-square triangles. Use 144 triangles for the Pansy blocks; use the remainder for the outer sawtooth border.

3 strips, each 2½" x 46"; crosscut into 54 squares, each 2½" x 2½"

From the remainder of the black fabric, cut the following strips from selvage to selvage (crosswise grain):

2 strips, each 2½" x 42"; crosscut into 6 segments, each 2½" x 12½", for sashing

2 strips, each 2⅞" x 42"; crosscut into 28 squares, each 2⅞" x 2⅞"; cut squares once diagonally to yield 56 half-square triangles for border

5 strips, each 2½" x 42", for binding

Directions

1. Following the block diagram below, arrange the squares and half-square triangles. Join the half-square triangles to make pieced squares. Join the squares and pieced squares in horizontal rows; press the seams in opposite directions from row to row. Join the rows to complete the blocks. Make 9 Pansy blocks.

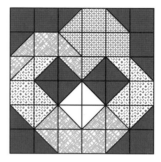

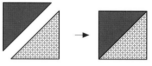

2. Assemble the blocks in 3 horizontal rows of 3 blocks each, adding short sashing strips between the blocks. Press the seams towards the sashing strips.

3. Measure the length of the horizontal rows of blocks. Cut 2 black 2½"-wide strips to that measurement. Sew the sashing strips between the rows of blocks.

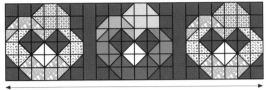

Measure

4. Following directions on pages 83–84 for straight-cut borders and using the remaining 2½"-wide black strips, measure, trim, and sew the inner border to the quilt.

5. Join the remaining pansy half-square triangles with a black half-square triangle to make pieced squares. Make a total of 92 pieced squares.

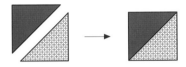

6. Join 22 pieced squares, arranging the squares as shown, to make each of the side border strips.

Make 2

7. Join 24 pieced squares, arranging the squares as shown, to make each of the top and bottom border strips. Notice the orientation of the pieced squares at each end.

Make 2

8. Sew the pieced border strips to the sides first, then to the top and bottom edges of the quilt. Place the pansy triangles toward the center of the quilt.

9. Layer the quilt with batting and backing; baste. Quilt as desired and bind the edges. We quilted in-the-ditch around each different print in the pansies and in a diagonal grid across the background and sashing.

10. Sign and date your quilt.

Sophisticated Strips

By Pam Lintott and Rosemary Miller

*Sophisticated Strips by Pam Lintott and Rosemary Miller, 1994,
Dorking, England, 50" x 78". Machine pieced and machine quilted.*

The most difficult thing about this quilt is choosing the fabric—you need five shades of two different colours—the rest is embarrassingly simple. This quilt is ideal for beginners and for those times when you need to create something especially fast.

Cambridge, England

Barbara Weiland

Materials: 44"-wide fabric

½ yd. black

1½ yds. charcoal

½ yd. dark grey

½ yd. grey

¼ yd. light grey

1¼ yds. maroon (includes binding)

¾ yd. deep pink

¾ yd. rose pink

¾ yd. pink

⅜ yd. pale pink

3⅛ yds. backing

Cutting

Cut strips across the width of the fabric.
All measurements include ¼"-wide seam allowances.

From each of the black, charcoal, dark grey, and grey fabrics, cut:
  12 strips, each 1¼" x 42"

From the light grey fabric, cut:
  6 strips, each 1¼" x 42"

From each of the maroon, deep pink, rose pink, and pink fabrics, cut:
  16 strips, each 1¼" x 42"

From the pale pink fabric, cut:
  8 strips, each 1¼" x 42"

From the charcoal fabric, cut:
  6 squares, each 12½" x 12½"; cut squares twice
    diagonally to yield quarter-square triangles for
    setting triangles
  2 squares, each 8¼" x 8¼"; cut squares once
    diagonally to yield half-square triangles for
    corner triangles

From the maroon fabric, cut:
  7 strips, each 2½" x 42", for binding

Directions

1. Make a strip unit by joining 2 each of the black, charcoal, dark grey, and grey strips and 1 of the light grey strips so that the colours gradate from black, to light grey, to black. Make a total of 6 strip units. Press the seams in one direction. It is essential to press the seams carefully since distortions can occur if pressed incorrectly. All seam allowances should lie flat and smooth. Refer to page 81 for pressing tips.

2. Make a strip unit by joining 2 each of the maroon, deep pink, rose pink, and pink strips and 1 of the pale pink strips so that colours gradate from maroon, to pale pink, to maroon. Make a total of 8 strip units. Press the seams in one direction.

3. Before cutting the strip units into squares, measure the width of your strip units. They should measure 7¼", but it doesn't matter if they are slightly narrower or wider. Cut the strip unit into squares, each 7¼" or the width of your strip units. For example, if your strip units measure only 7", cut them into 7" squares. Cut 40 squares from the maroon/pink strip units, and 28 squares from the black/grey strip units. You should be able to cut 5 squares from each strip unit.

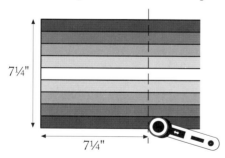

4. Starting in the upper left corner with a pink block, sew the blocks in diagonal rows as shown below. Increase each row by 2 blocks, alternating pink and black blocks until Row 5. Repeat Row 5 three more times (rows 6, 7, and 8) to obtain the length of the quilt and then decrease the remaining rows by 2 blocks each until you reach the bottom right corner.

5. Join the setting triangles to the end of each row, then join the rows. Add the corner triangles last. Refer to Tip Box at right for assembling diagonally set quilts. The setting and corner triangles are oversized and will be trimmed slightly in the next step.

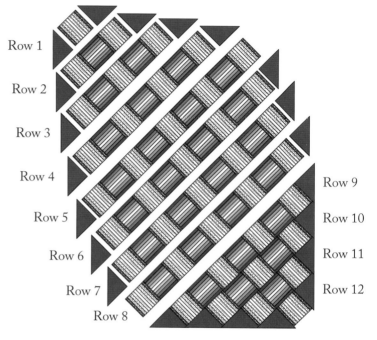

6. To straighten the edges of the quilt, align the 1¼" line on the ruler with the block points. Use a rotary cutter to trim the excess fabric along the edge of the ruler.

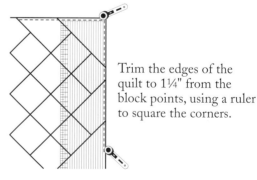

Trim the edges of the quilt to 1¼" from the block points, using a ruler to square the corners.

7. Layer the quilt with batting and backing; baste. Quilt as desired and bind the edges. We machine quilted circles, using a 10" dinner plate to mark the design.

8. Sign and date your quilt.

Setting Blocks On Point

A block can take on a totally new look when set on point. It can make even the simplest block look complex. Just a few things need to be considered when planning your quilt.

1. Fewer blocks are needed than when a quilt is set straight. To calculate the measurements of your quilt, you need to know the measurement of the block from point to point. To calculate this, multiply the size of the finished block by 1.414. For example, a 6" square block measures approximately 8½" on the diagonal (6 x 1.414 = 8.48 ; round up to 8.5).

2. Arrange the blocks on point as desired or follow the quilt plan for the quilt you are making. Starting at one corner, sew the blocks together in diagonal rows. The first row has one block, and every row then increases by two blocks until you reach the desired width of the quilt. Repeat the longest row to reach the desired length of the quilt, then decrease each row by two blocks until you reach the corner or last row, which has only one block.

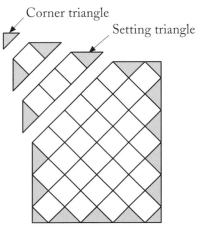

Assembly Diagram for On-Point Set

3. Add setting triangles to the end of each row to complete the rows. To keep the outside edges of your quilt on the straight of grain, you must use quarter-square triangles, that is, a square cut twice diagonally to yield 4 triangles. To calculate the size square to cut, calculate the diagonal measurement of your block (see step 1 above) and add

1¼". Match the square corners of the triangle and the block and start sewing from the corner as shown.

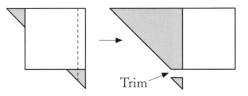

Trim

4. Add the four corners last. To ensure that the outside edges of your quilt are on the straight of grain, you must use half-square triangles, that is, a square cut once diagonally to yield two triangles. To calculate the size square to cut, divide the finished size of your block by 1.414 and then add ⅞". Match the centre of the triangle to the centre of the square and sew from edge to edge as shown.

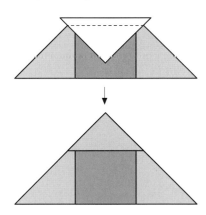

Note: Sometimes setting and corner triangles are cut oversized so that the blocks appear to float on the background. Edges are straightened before borders are added.

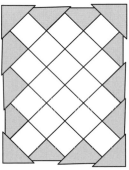

All Square Quilt

BY JOAN TAYLOR

All Square Quilt by Joan Taylor 1994, Reigate, England, 94½" x 94½". Machine pieced and hand quilted.

Joan had a number of 2" squares left over from a previous quilt and was trying to decide what to do with them. While she was playing around with the pieces, the central block emerged and the quilt just grew from there. Using graph paper, she drew up one-quarter of the design and coloured it, then followed her design to make four quarters. There are 3,481 squares in the entire quilt.

Materials: 44"-wide fabric

2⅜ yds. dark blue (includes outer border)

⅞ yd. blue floral

⅝ yd. paisley

2¼ yds. dark pink (includes inner border)

¾ yd. light pink

4⅜ yds. calico

⅞ yd. binding

8⅛ yds. backing

Cutting

Cut strips across the width of the fabric.
All measurements include ¼"-wide seam allowances.
Cut all squares 2" x 2". You can cut
378 squares from 1 yard of fabric.

No. of Squares	Fabric
792	Dark blue
288	Blue floral
192	Paisley
396	Dark pink
232	Light pink
1581	Calico

From the dark blue fabric, cut:
    9 strips, each 2" x 42", for outer border
From the dark pink fabric, cut:
    9 strips, each 2" x 42", for inner border
From the binding fabric, cut:
    10 strips, each 2½" x 42"

Houses of Parliament across the Thames

Directions

1. Arrange the 2" squares, following the quilt diagram below to make Quarter 1. Add the Centre 1 and 2 rows to Quarter 1.

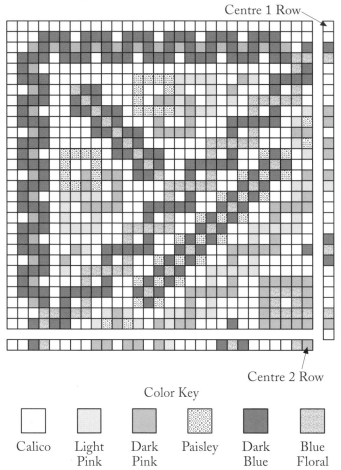

Centre 1 Row

Centre 2 Row

Color Key

Calico	Light Pink	Dark Pink	Paisley	Dark Blue	Blue Floral

2. Chain piece the squares in vertical rows. Chain piece vertical Rows 1 and 2 together and label these rows. Next, chain piece Row 3 to Row 2 and again label it. Following the diagram, continue in this manner until all the vertical rows of Quarter 1 are pieced together. It is not necessary to cut the threads between the squares. Do not press the seams yet.

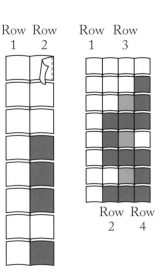

Row 1 Row 2   Row 1 Row 3

Row 2 Row 4

3. Now the fun begins. Sew all the rows together, making sure the seams go in the opposite directions and that they butt together well. Now press the Quarter 1 section of your quilt.

4. Repeat steps 1, 2, and 3 to make the other three quarter sections of the quilt. Except add only a Centre 2 row to the right side of Quarter 2, and Quarter 3. Quarter 4 does not have an additional centre row.

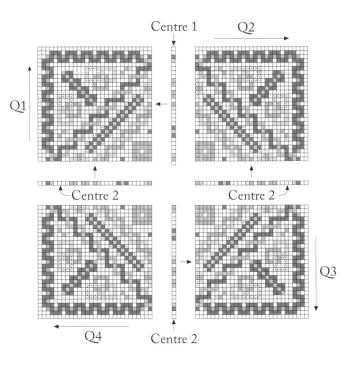

Centre 1   Q2

Q1

Centre 2   Centre 2

Q4   Centre 2

Q3

5. Sew Quarter 1 to Quarter 2, and Quarter 3 to Quarter 4, rotating the quarters as necessary to form the pattern. Then join the halves together.

6. Following directions on pages 83–84 for straight-cut borders, measure, cut, and sew the inner border strips to the quilt. Repeat with the outer border.

7. Layer the quilt with batting and backing; baste. Quilt as desired and bind the edges. Joan hand quilted in both diagonal and straight lines.

8. Sign and date your quilt.

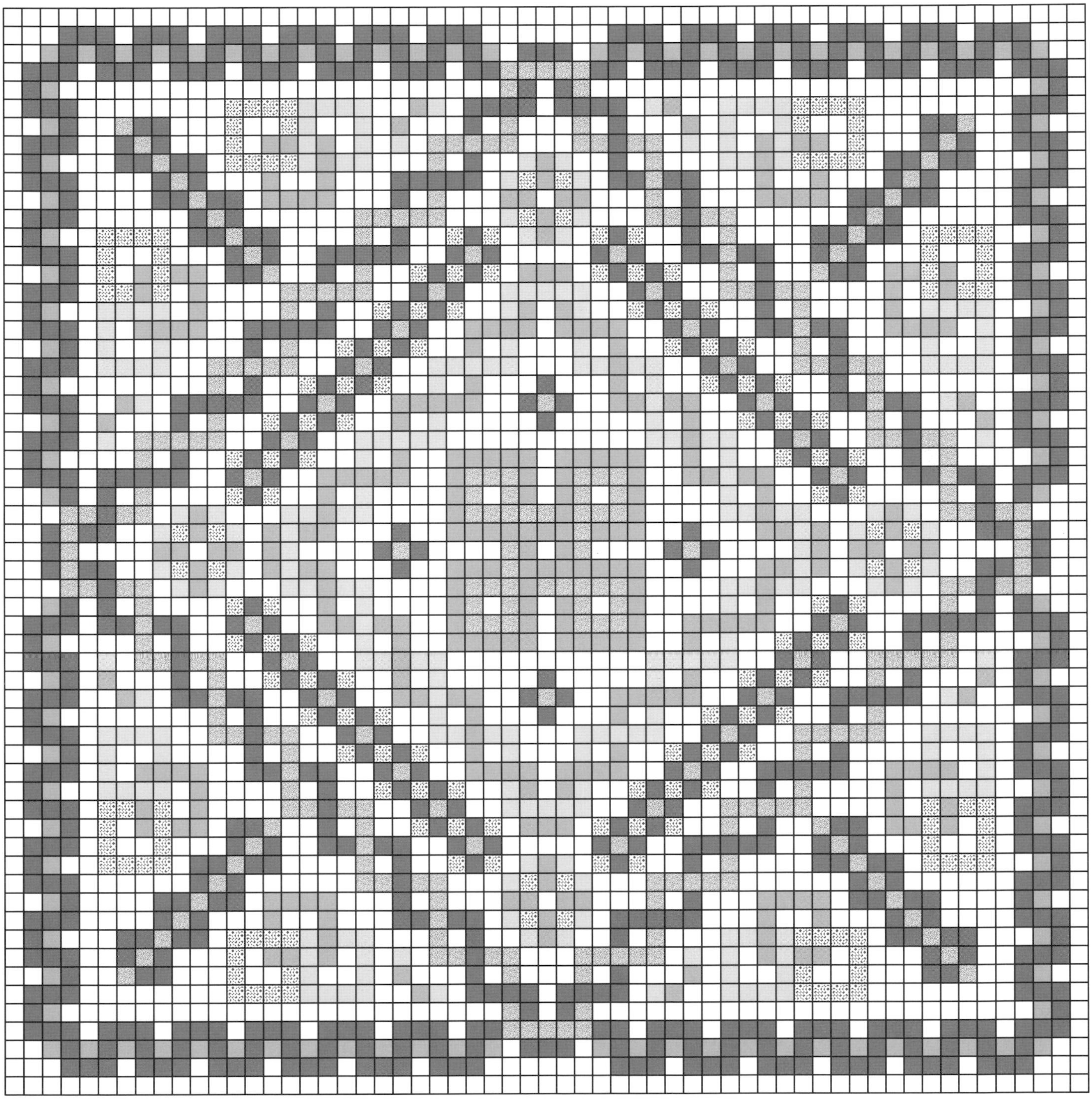

Victorian Memories

BY CAROLYN FORSTER

*Victorian Memories by Carolyn Forster, 1993, Tunbridge Wells, England, 80" x 80".
Machine pieced, hand appliquéd, and hand quilted.*

Carolyn wanted to make a quilt reminiscent of those from the 1800s. She spent a few months researching quilts from this period and visited the quilt collection at the Victoria and Albert Museum, where the staff was most helpful. Carolyn spent longer researching the project than actually putting it together (but not quilting it!). These quilts, often referred to as medallion quilts, incorporated both pieced patchwork and appliqué but were not always quilted.

One of the appliqué techniques popular at the time was broderie perse. Ladies would cut small motifs from hard-to-come-by Indian chintzes and arrange them on a large background to make a new design. The motifs were then appliquéd to the background with a buttonhole or herringbone stitch to cover the raw edges. Traditional appliqué on a plain background was also used. Carolyn used broderie perse for the centre of the quilt and traditional appliqué for the borders.

The pieced patchwork often consisted of large, simple shapes: squares and triangles. The primary function of the patchwork was to show off the appliqué in the centre of the quilt. Dress fabrics and furnishing scraps were used extensively.

Elaborate quilting was not prevalent at this time, and often batting was not used between the top and the backing. Carolyn chose to quilt the top and used a cotton batting (Hobbs Heirloom) to give the finished quilt an old-fashioned flat look. She used simple shapes and lots of outline quilting to enhance the appliqué and patchwork.

Making this quilt is an excellent way to use up fabrics from your scrap bag. To give the quilt an old-fashioned look, Carolyn selected fabrics with antique tones. You can also overdye fabrics with tea to gain this effect. For a more authentic feel, Carolyn chose small floral prints, woven checks and plaids, large-scale furnishing prints, toile de jouy, and glazed cotton chintzes.

Materials: 44"-wide fabric

2¾ yds. background

¼ -½ yd. glazed cotton chintz print for centre motifs*

1 yd. border print

2½ yds. green for vines and leaves

1¼ yds. total assorted light prints

1¼ yds. total assorted dark prints

½ yd. paper-backed fusible web

⅝ yd. binding

4¾ yds. backing

*The amount of yardage will vary, depending on the print fabric selected.

Directions

*Cutting and assembly instructions are combined below
for the quilt centre and for each of the four borders.
All measurements include ¼"-wide seam allowances.
Use templates on pullout pattern.*

Quilt Centre

1. **From the background fabric, cut:**
   1 square, 23⅛" x 23⅛"
   From the glazed cotton chintz print, cut:
   flowers, birds, leaves as desired for the centre medallion (Leave at least ½" around the shapes.)

2. Cut out pieces of paper-backed fusible web to match
   the motif shapes. Iron these shapes to the wrong side
   of the motifs.

3. Trim the motifs to the desired size, either exactly on
   the outline of the design or ⅛" to 3/16" around the
   edge of the design if you want the background surrounding the design to show just a bit. You do not
   need to add a seam allowance, since the motifs will
   be ironed in place.

4. Arrange the motifs on the
   background square in a
   well-balanced design.
   Gently peel the paper
   backing from the motifs
   and iron them in place.

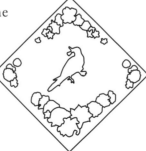

5. Use a buttonhole or closed herringbone stitch to sew
   around each motif, covering the raw edges and secur-
   ing the design to the background square. Use buttonhole twist or stranded embroidery cotton or silk
   thread in a colour to match the background or the
   colour in the motifs. You may want to use an embroidery hoop to steady the work and keep it flat.

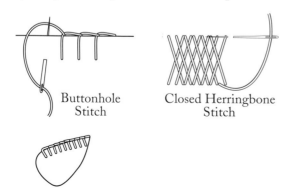

Buttonhole   Closed Herringbone
Stitch   Stitch

Note: If you prefer to use the broderie perse method
without the use of a paper-backed fusible web; cut
shapes as desired, pin or baste in place, and appliqué
using buttonhole or herringbone stitch.

Pieced Corner Triangles

1. **From background fabric, cut:**
   16 squares, each 2⅞" x 2⅞"; cut squares once
   diagonally to yield 32 half-square triangles
   36 squares, each 2½" x 2½"
   From assorted light and dark prints, cut:
   48 squares, each 2½" x 2½"

2. Join the squares and half-square triangles in rows as
   shown. Press the seams towards the assorted print
   squares. Join the rows together to make a large corner triangle. Make 4 corner triangles.

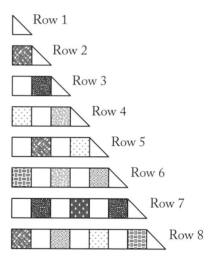

Row 1
Row 2
Row 3
Row 4
Row 5
Row 6
Row 7
Row 8

3. Join the triangles to each side of the centre square to
   make the centre of the quilt.

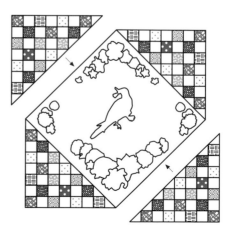

First Border

1. **From the border print fabric, cut:**
   4 strips, each 4½" x 32½"
   From the background fabric, cut:
   8 squares, each 2½" x 2½"
   From the assorted light and dark prints, cut:
   8 squares, each 2½" x 2½"
2. Join 2 background squares and 2 print squares to make a four-patch unit. Make 4 units.

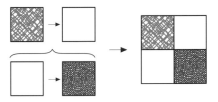

3. Sew 2 of the border strips to the top and bottom of the centre panel.

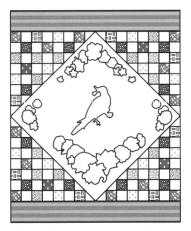

4. Join a four-patch unit to each end of the remaining border strips and sew to each side of the centre panel.

Second Border

APPLIQUÉ VINE PANEL

1. **From the background fabric, cut:**
   4 rectangles, each 8½" x 40½"
   From green fabric, cut:
   10 yds. of bias strips, 1¼" wide
   68 of Template #1
   From assorted light and dark prints, cut:
   4 of Template #2
   8 of Template #3
   12 of Template #4
   4 of Template #5
   12 of Template #6
   20 of Template #7
   20 of Template #8
   4 of Template #9
   16 of Template #10
   4 of Template #11
2. Join the ends of the green bias strips to make one long continuous strip. Press the strip in half with wrong sides together.

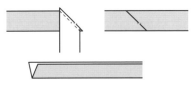

3. Trace the two sections of the appliquéd vine pattern on the pullout pattern insert onto one sheet of paper. Place a background rectangle on top of the traced vine pattern. Use a pencil to lightly trace the design onto the rectangle.
4. Pin the raw edges of the bias strip along the drawn line, leaving at least 4" at either end. The ends will be appliquéd onto the corner blocks. Cut 5 lengths of bias strip, each approximately 6", for the flower stems. Pin the stems in place with one end tucked under the main vine. The other end will be covered by a flower or bud.

5. Beginning with the flower stems, hand stitch the stems to the background with a running stitch, ¼" from the raw edges.

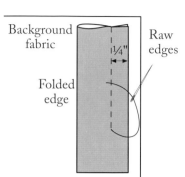

6. Turn the folded edge to cover the running stitch and raw edges. Slipstitch the folded edge in place. Repeat with all stems and then with the long vine.

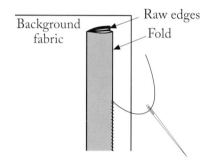

7. Pin the flowers and leaves in place, making sure to cover the raw ends of the flower stems. Use either the needle-turn technique or freezer-paper technique to appliqué the flowers and leaves. See pages 82–83 for appliqué techniques. Make 4 appliqué panels.

Star Corner Block

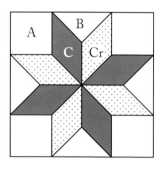

1. **From the background fabric, cut:**
   16 of Template A
   16 of Template B
   From the assorted light and dark prints, cut:
   16 of Template C
   16 of Template C reversed

2. Join C and Cr in pairs, stitching from the centre to within ¼" of the inside corner; backstitch. Make 4 pairs.

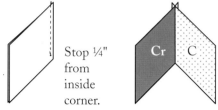

3. Join 2 pairs to make half of a star, again stitching from the centre to within ¼" of the inside corner; backstitch.

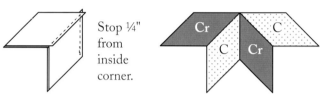

4. Insert 1 triangle (piece B) and 2 squares (piece A) to each half star.

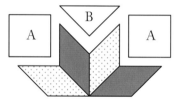

Beginning with the triangle, mark the inside corner of the triangle on the wrong side of the fabric. Match the mark to the inside corner between the 2 diamonds. With raw edges aligned, stitch from the outer edge to ¼" from the inside corner; backstitch. Pin the other side of the triangle to the adjacent diamond and stitch from the outer edge to within ¼" of the inside corner. Press the triangle towards the diamonds.

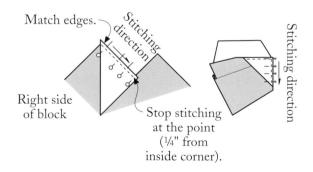

5. Mark one corner of a square ¼" from the edges on the wrong side of the fabric. Match the mark to the inside corner between the 2 diamonds. With raw edges aligned, stitch from the outer edge to ¼" from the inside corner; backstitch. Pin the other side of the square to the adjacent diamond and stitch from the outer edge to within ¼" of the inside corner. Press the squares towards the diamonds.

6. Pin 2 star halves together and sew from one side to the other, starting and stopping ¼" from the inside corners. Make sure to match the points at the centre of the star. Insert the remaining triangles as described above in step 4. Press the seam open to reduce bulk. Make 4 stars.

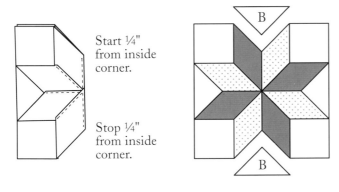

Assembling the Second Border

1. Join an appliqué vine panel to the top and bottom edges of the quilt centre. Sew a star corner block to each end of the remaining appliqué panels; do not stitch the end of the vine into the seam. Sew a border strip to each side of the quilt centre.

2. Appliqué the extra length of vine onto the corner block. Fold the raw ends under or undo a few stitches in the seam allowances of the star and tuck the ends inside; close the seam allowance. The vine should look as though it continues around the corner, under the star and into the next panel.

Third Border

1. **From the background fabric, cut:**
   4 squares, each 4½" x 4½"
   From the light assorted prints, cut:
   28 squares, each 4⅞" x 4⅞"; cut squares once diagonally to yield 56 light half-square triangles
   From the dark assorted prints, cut:
   28 squares, each 4⅞" x 4⅞"; cut squares once diagonally to yield 56 dark half-square triangles

2. Join a light triangle and a dark triangle to make a pieced square.

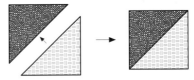

3. Join 14 squares, arranging the squares as shown, to make each of the 4 pieced border strips.

Top and Bottom Borders
Make 2

Side Borders
Make 2

4. Join the top and bottom border strips to the top and bottom edges of the quilt. Notice the position of the diagonal seam in the pieced squares at either end of the pieced border strips. Rotate the border strips as necessary to match the diagram below. Add a background square to each end of the side pieced border strips and sew to each side of the quilt, again rotating the border strip as necessary to match the diagram.

Fourth Border

1. **From the background fabric, cut:**
   4 squares, each 8½" x 8½"
   8 of Template D

2. Join 2 triangles to an 8½" square as shown to make a corner piece. Press the seam allowances towards the square.

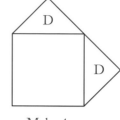

Make 4

3. **From the green fabric, cut:**
   6 yds. of bias strips, 1¼" wide
   60 of Template #12

4. Pin the curved stems and vines and appliqué as described in steps 4–6 on pages 41–42. Pin the leaves in place and appliqué. Be careful not to appliqué the leaves into the ¼"-wide seam allowances.

5. **From the background fabric, cut:**
   4 of Template E
   From the green fabric, cut:
   16 of Template #12
   From the assorted light and dark prints, cut:
   4 of Template #13
   4 of Template #14
   16 of Template #15

6. Appliqué the stems, flowers, and leaves onto the background square. Refer to the Placement Guide on the pullout pattern. Be careful not to appliqué the leaves into the ¼"-wide seam allowance.

7. **From the light assorted prints, cut:**
   24 of Template E
   From the dark assorted prints, cut:
   32 matching pairs of Template D (for a total of 64)

8. Arrange the corner units, light squares, appliquéd squares, and pairs of matching dark triangles around the quilt as shown.

Matching triangles

9. Sew the pieces in units as shown; then join the units to complete the rows. Make 4 rows. There are 8 triangles that will not be sewn as part of the row.

10. Sew the remaining triangles to each corner unit as shown. Be sure to use the appropriate triangle with the appropriate corner unit.

11. Join pieced border strips to the sides of the quilt. Add the corner units last.

12. Layer the quilt with batting and backing; baste. Quilt as desired or follow the quilting suggestion. Cut 9 strips, each 2½" wide, and bind the edges.

13. Sign and date your quilt.

Pinewood Quilt

BY JOAN TAYLOR

Pinewood Quilt by Joan Taylor, 1993, Reigate, England, 74" x 84". Machine pieced and hand quilted.

Joan loves to use up scraps and is always adapting and altering patterns. Her quilts resemble the colourful garden and the woods surrounding her house. The orange in this quilt represents the sunlight in the dark woods, and the pale border the daylight outside the woods.

The idea behind Pinewood Quilt was to make it asymmetrical, so a rectangular block was used. The quilt was not planned and grew from the middle outwards, but somehow, despite the intentions, it became more symmetrical as it progressed.

We have simplified the design and construction of this quilt. For this reason, it does not exactly match the photo. Feel free, however, to play with the blocks as Joan did and create your own design.

Materials: 44"-wide fabric

4¼ yds. total light fabrics

3⅛ yds. total dark fabrics
(include medium dark and very dark fabrics)

1 yd. outer border

¾ yd. binding

4½ yds. backing

Cutting

The chart below indicates the number of pieces required to make one block, and the total number of pieces required to make all the blocks in this quilt.

	A Block		B Block	
	1 block	60 blocks	1 block	32 blocks
Piece A	1	60	2	64
Piece B	6	360	4	128
Piece C	7	420	6	192

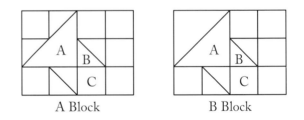

A Block   B Block

You can cut the pieces using templates found on page 51, or follow the instructions below for rotary cutting the pieces.

All measurements include ¼"-wide seam allowances.

For Piece A, cut squares 4⅜" x 4⅜";
  cut the squares once diagonally to yield large half-square triangles.

For Piece B, cut squares 2⅝" x 2⅝";
  cut the squares once diagonally to yield small half-square triangles.

For Piece C, cut squares, 2¼" x 2¼".

From the outer border fabric, cut:
  8 strips, each 4" x 42".

From the binding fabric, cut:
  9 strips, each 2½" x 42".

Westminster Abbey

Claudia L'Heureux

Third Pieced Border   Ninepatch Blocks   A Block   First Pieced Border   B Block

Directions

1. Using an assortment of fabrics in each block, arrange the pieces. Join the half-square triangles to make pieced squares. Following the piecing diagrams, join the pieces.

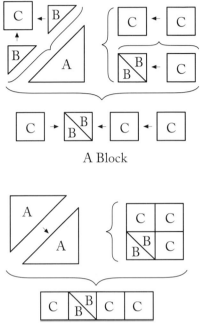

A Block

B Block

Note: In our quilt, 39 of the A blocks have only assorted dark fabrics. Seven have only assorted light fabrics, and the remaining 14 have a combination of dark and light fabrics. The B blocks all have assorted light fabrics. Make your blocks in similar colour combinations or use your own combinations to create a unique design.

2. Join the A blocks in 10 rows of 6 blocks each. Press the seams in opposite directions from row to row. Join the rows.

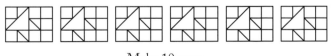

Make 10 rows.

3. Using 3 very dark squares and 6 light squares, follow the piecing diagram to make a Ninepatch block. Make 8 blocks.

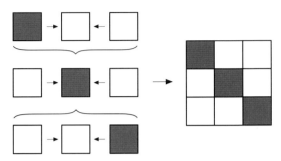

4. The first pieced border is made up of 3 rows of 2¼" squares. Use very dark squares for Row 1, medium dark squares for Row 2, and light squares for Row 3.

   From assorted very dark fabrics, cut:
   108 squares, each 2¼" x 2¼"

   From assorted medium dark fabrics, cut:
   108 squares, each 2¼" x 2¼"

   From assorted light fabrics, cut:
   108 squares, each 2¼" x 2¼"

5. Join the squares into rows; press the seam allowances in opposite directions from row to row. Join the rows as shown below.

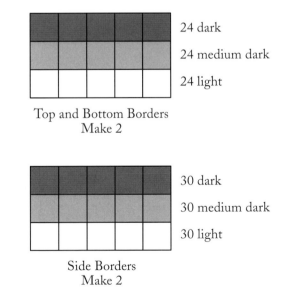

Top and Bottom Borders
Make 2

Side Borders
Make 2

6. Sew a side border strip to each side of the quilt. Add a Ninepatch block to each end of the top and bottom border strips, orienting the dark squares as shown. Sew to the top and bottom edges of the quilt.

7. Join 9 B blocks for each of the side border strips and sew to each side of the quilt. Notice the orientation of the A triangles in each border strip.

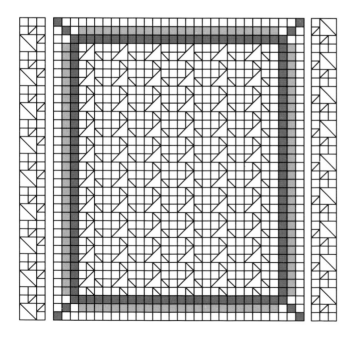

8. Join 3 light squares in a vertical row. Make 4.

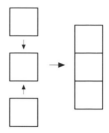

9. Join 7 B blocks, 2 Ninepatch blocks, and 2 rows of light squares to make the top and bottom border strips. Be sure to orient the dark squares in the Ninepatch block as shown. Sew to the top and bottom edges of the quilt.

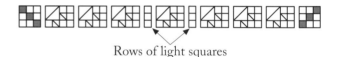

Rows of light squares

10. The third pieced border is a single row of dark squares.
   From assorted dark fabrics, cut:
      156 squares, each 2¼" x 2¼"
   From a very dark fabric, cut:
      4 squares, each 2¼" x 2¼"

11. Join 42 squares for each of the side border strips. Sew a side border strip to each side of the quilt.

12. Join 36 dark squares for each of the top and bottom border strips. Add a very dark square to each end of the border strips; sew to the top and bottom edges of the quilt.

13. Following directions on pages 83–84 for straight-cut borders, measure, cut, and sew the 4" outer border strips to the quilt.

14. Layer the quilt with batting and backing; baste. Quilt as desired and bind the edges. Joan quilted a series of circles on the light fabrics to suggest the sun, and the rest of the quilting radiates from this in straight lines.

15. Sign and date your quilt.

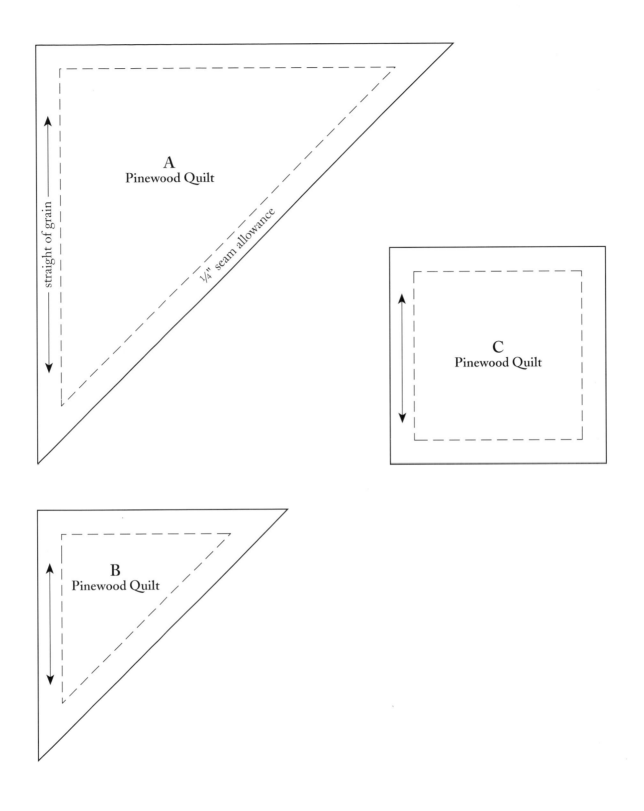

A
Pinewood Quilt

straight of grain

¼" seam allowance

C
Pinewood Quilt

B
Pinewood Quilt

Cream on Cream

BY MARGARET HUGHES

Cream on Cream by Margaret Hughes, 1993, Bookham, England, 25½" x 32".
Hand appliquéd with a hand-pieced patchwork border. Hand quilted.

We had hoped to capture Margaret in action—no, we don't mean quilting but one of her other hobbies—tap dancing! Who says quilters are crazy? Margaret loves handwork and this wall hanging uses the technique of broderie perse, which is a form of appliqué dating back to the seventeenth century.

Margaret's Cream on Cream quilt features a vase brimming with flowers surrounded by a patchwork border. The directions for this quilt have been modified slightly for easier construction. For this reason, it does not exactly match the quilt in the photo.

Materials: 44"-wide fabric

½ yd. background

¼ yd. light blue

¼ yd. medium blue

⅜ yd. light floral print*

¼ yd. medium floral print*

¼ yd. dark floral print*

½ yd. peach (includes inner and outer borders)

Scrap large enough for the vase
(approximately 6" x 8")

½ yd. binding

1 yd. backing

*You may need additional yardage if you want to cut specific leaf and flower motifs from the floral prints. You may also want to buy more floral prints if you want to include different types and colours of flowers in your arrangement.

Tower Bridge

Cutting

Cut strips across the width of the fabric.
All measurements include ¼"-wide seam allowances.

Note: Before cutting the squares and triangles from the floral prints, cut the leaves and flowers for your arrangement first, so that you do not cut into a motif that you might want. See step 3 on page 55.

From the background fabric, cut:
    1 rectangle, 11⅜" x 15¾"

From the light blue fabric, cut:
    2 strips, each 3⅜" x 42"; crosscut into 21 squares, each 3⅜" x 3⅜"; cut the squares twice diagonally to yield 84 quarter-square triangles

From the medium blue fabric, cut:
    2 strips, each 2⅜" x 42"; crosscut into 19 squares, each 2⅜" x 2⅜"; cut the squares once diagonally to yield 38 half-square triangles

From the light floral print, cut:
    42 squares, each 2" x 2"

From the medium floral print, cut:
    19 squares, each 2⅜" x 2⅜"; cut the squares once diagonally to yield 38 half-square triangles

From the dark floral print, cut:
    46 squares, each 2" x 2"

From the peach fabric, cut:
    2 strips, each 3½" x 21¾", for inner side border
    2 strips, each 2½" x 15⅜", for inner top and bottom border
    4 strips, each 1¼" x 42", for outer border

From the binding fabric, cut:
    4 strips, each 3⅛" x 42"

Color Key

Background   Light blue   Medium blue   Peach   Light floral print   Medium floral print   Dark floral print

Directions

1. Using the vase pattern on the pullout pattern, cut the shape from the vase fabric.

2. Position it on the lower half of the background rectangle and appliqué around the sides and bottom edges. It isn't necessary to stitch the top of the vase because it will be covered by flowers. (See directions on page 82 for needle-turn appliqué.)

3. Cut out the flowers, leaves, etc., from your floral prints. Leave at least ½" around the shapes. Follow steps 2–5 on page 40 to prepare and appliqué the motifs.

4. Sew the 3½"-wide inner border strips to the sides of the quilt first. Then sew the 2½"-wide strips to the top and bottom edges. Press the seams towards the border strips.

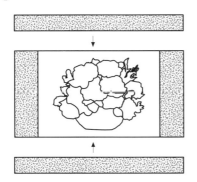

5. Join the blue triangles and medium floral print triangles to make pieced squares. Arrange the pieced squares, background triangles, and the light and dark floral squares as shown below to make 2 border strips for the sides and 2 border strips for the top and bottom edges. Join the pieces in diagonal rows, then join the rows.

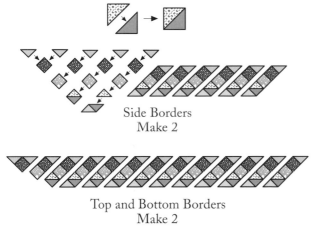

Side Borders
Make 2

Top and Bottom Borders
Make 2

6. With rights sides facing, pin the long edge of one of the border strips to the quilt. Start and stop stitching ¼" from each corner of the quilt; backstitch at each end. Repeat with remaining border strips. Press the seams towards the inner border so that the pieced border will lie flat.

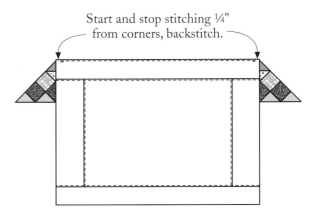

Start and stop stitching ¼" from corners, backstitch.

7. To mitre the corners, turn the quilt over and match the diagonal raw edges of the borders together. Pin the edges, making sure to match the seams. Stitch from the inside corner to the outer edge. Press the seams open.

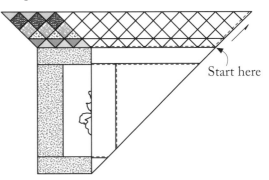

Start here

8. Following directions on pages 83–84 for straight-cut borders, measure, cut, and sew the outer border strips to the quilt top.

9. Layer the quilt with batting and backing; baste. Quilt as desired. To make a wider binding, cut the strips 3⅛" and attach to the quilt, using a ½"-wide seam allowance. Follow directions on pages 86–87 for binding the quilt, but remember to use a ½"-wide seam allowance instead of a ¼"-wide seam allowance.

10. Sign and date your quilt.

Star Turn

BY EDYTH HENRY

*Star Turn by Edyth Henry, 1994, Lymington, England, 28" x 33". This quilt was inspired
by Deirdre Amsden's Colourwash technique. Hand pieced and machine quilted using
981 of the fabric samples from The Quilt Room's 1993/94 Sample Pack.*

In 1993 when, for the first time, The Quilt Room sample pack numbered 1,000 fabrics, Edyth decided it was a wonderful opportunity to make a Charm quilt without the problem of collecting fabrics.

Edyth wanted to try Deirdre Amsden's Colourwash technique. In many of Deirdre's quilts, part of the centre is reversed. The theme for Quilts United Kingdom, 1994, was Star quilts, so Edyth decided she could reverse a star in the middle of her colourwash. Finally, she chose the very basic method of English paper piecing.

Cutting and covering 1,000 hexagons took Edyth about a month. She worked in odd moments during the day and for perhaps an hour in the evening.

For the next stage, Edyth arranged them in 37 rows of 27 hexagons, with light ones at the top and dark ones at the bottom. This took 999 of her 1000 hexagons, leaving one to spare. She then removed 18 hexagons from the right-hand side to make the quilt symmetrical, thus using only 981 pieces in the quilt and leaving a total of 19 spares.

As you can imagine, Edyth spent some time arranging and rearranging the pieces, trying to get a smooth colourwash. She had trouble with the yellows and oranges in the sample pack because they just would not blend with the other fabrics, so she pulled them all out and used them to form a star—the focal point in the centre.

Editor's Note: Because of the small size of the pieces in the sample pack, Edyth could only use a hexagon that measured 1.5cm or .59 inches on each side. For those not wanting to deal with so small a template, we have provided 2 additional hexagons in a larger size.

Materials

981 pieces of fabric at least ¼" larger all around than the size of the hexagon template (page 59) you choose.

½ yd. border fabric

Guard at Buckingham Palace

Directions

1. Make a cardboard or plastic template of one of the hexagons on page 59. Cut 981 hexagon shapes from lightweight cardstock or freezer paper.

2. Pin a paper hexagon to the wrong side of a small piece of fabric; or, if you are using freezer-paper hexagons, iron them to the wrong side of the fabric. Cut around the shape, leaving a ¼"-wide seam allowance all around.

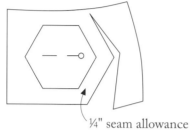

¼" seam allowance

3. Fold the ¼"-wide seam allowance over the edge of the paper and baste.

4. Following the diagram below, arrange the covered hexagons to make a star or a design of your own choosing.

5. To make assembling the 981 hexagons a bit more manageable, sew the hexagons for the centre star into equilateral triangles. There are 12 triangles, each one made up of 36 hexagons, with 8 hexagons on each side of the triangle.

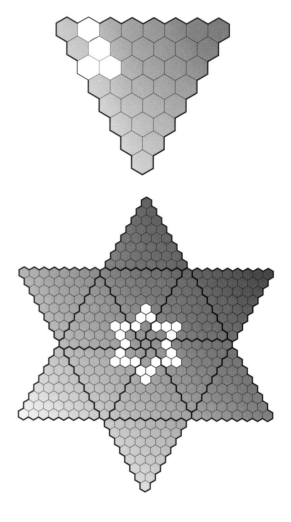

Whipstitch the hexagons together as shown to make the triangles. Join the triangles to the centre hexagon to complete the star.

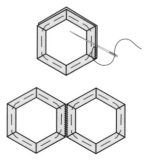

6. Sew the background hexagons into position around the star.
7. From the border fabric, cut 4 strips, each 4" x 42". Centring a border on one side, pin or baste the border under the edge of the pieced hexagon quilt top, so that the border extends about 2" beyond the hexagons as shown. There should be an equal amount of border fabric at each end of the quilt side. Repeat with the other 3 sides of the quilt.

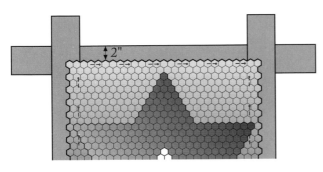

8. Mitre the corners of the borders, following directions on page 85. Appliqué the edges of the outer hexagons to the border fabric.

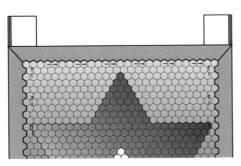

9. Remove all the papers and give the quilt top a good pressing.
10. Layer the quilt top with batting and backing; baste. Star Turn was machine quilted with swirling lines, emphasizing the movement of the star, and straight lines, echoing the star shape on the background. A final row of machine quilting was added around the edge of the hexagons in the border. You can use the traditional method to bind the edges (pages 86–87) or simply turn the edge of the border to the back side, fold under the 1/4"-wide seam allowance, and blindstitch by hand.
11. Sign and date your quilt.

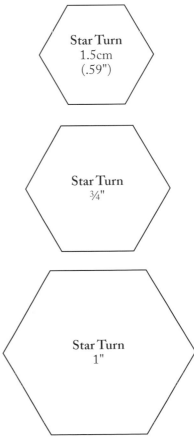

Star Turn
1.5cm
(.59")

Star Turn
3/4"

Star Turn
1"

Japanese Sunrise

GROUP QUILT BY DOWNSIDE QUILTERS

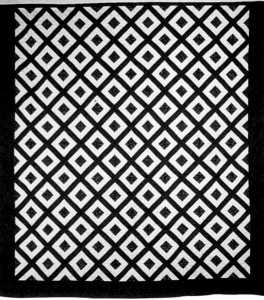

Japanese Sunrise by Downside Quilters, 1993, Guildford, England, 80" x 90". Hand pieced and hand quilted.

PikeRiver Films Limited

PikeRiver Films Limited

Reverse of Japanese Sunrise ➙

Cutting

Cut strips across the width of the fabric.
All measurements include ¼"-wide seam allowances.

From each of the 3 black prints, cut:
45 strips, each 2" x 42", for a total of 135 strips

From the white-on-white print, cut:
90 strips, each 2" x 42"

From the assorted shades of solid yellow fabric, cut:
224 squares, each 5" x 5"

From each of the black border fabrics, cut:
4 strips, each 5½" x 80½"

From the low-loft batting, cut:
4 strips, each 5" x 80", for borders
224 squares, each 5" x 5"

The Downside Quilters of Guildford produced this fantastic quilt, using the technique of Japanese folded patchwork. The quilt is reversible, with a delightful flowerlike effect on the front and an eye-catching geometric design on the back. The striking design on the reverse of this quilt was not planned. One of the members, Chris Reid, came up with the idea of using black and white strips for the backing, and it was only when starting the final assembly of the quilt that the striking design became apparent. Not a bad bonus! We would like to thank the Downside Quilters for allowing us to use their quilt and to Jean Davidson and Margot Abrahams for their help in writing these instructions.

Materials: 44"-wide fabric

2⅝ yds. each of 3 different black prints

5¼ yds. white-on-white print

4 yds. total assorted shades of solid yellow

6¼ yds. low-loft batting (36" wide)

2⅜ yds. each of 2 different black fabrics for seamless front and back borders

Detail of gate at Buckingham Palace

Directions

1. Join 3 different black-print strips and 2 white-on-white strips to make a strip unit as shown. Press the seams towards the black prints. Make 45 strip units.

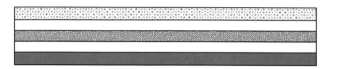

2. Make a plastic template of the 7¾" circle on the pullout pattern. Mark the centre line on your template. Aligning the centre line of the circle with the middle of the centre black strip, trace circles on the strip units. Cut the circles out on the drawn lines. You should get 5 circles per strip unit. Cut a total of 224 circles.

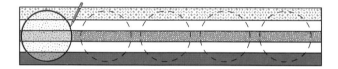

3. Carefully turn under a scant ¼"-wide seam allowance around the circumference of the circle and baste.

4. Lay the striped circle right side down and position a 5" square of batting and a 5" yellow square right side up in the middle as shown. Pin in position. Great care should be taken when positioning the square onto the striped circle. The diagonal of the square must line up with the centre of the middle stripe of the circle to ensure the formation of the flower pattern on the front and the square box pattern on the reverse of the quilt.

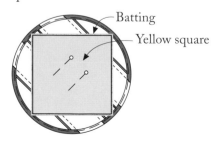

Batting
Yellow square

5. Fold the edges of the circle over the square and pin as shown.

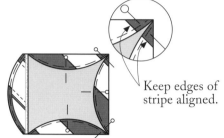

Keep edges of stripe aligned.

Pin across each corner and edge.

6. Quilt each arc of the circle in place, ⅛" from the folded edge. Remove the basting stitches. Add a second row of quilting on the inside of the square, ⅛" from the folded edge of each arc.

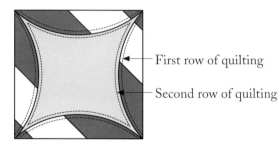

First row of quilting
Second row of quilting

Make 224 blocks.

7. To join the blocks, pin 2 blocks together with right sides facing. Whipstitch the ends securely. Join 14 blocks to make one row. Make 16 rows. Join the rows, whipstitching the seams securely between the rows.

Front

Back

Note: Sew the blocks together very firmly since the finished quilt is extremely heavy. Learn from the experience of the Downside Quilters. When they held up the quilt for the first time, the weight caused the seams to part slightly, and daylight showed through. The entire quilt had to be resewn but, this time, with serious stitching! Fortunately, the group's sense of humour stood the test.

8. To make the tubular borders, place one length of the front and back borders together with right sides facing. Machine sew along one long edge, ¼" from the raw edges.

9. Turn the border so that the right sides are facing out. Place a 5" length of batting in between the front and back border. Turn the ¼"-wide seam allowances of the raw edges towards the inside of the tube and hand stitch the remaining long edge closed, catching the batting in the seam to hold it in place. Don't forget to close the ends as well. Make 4 border strips

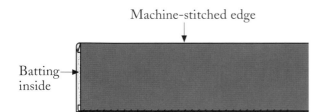

Machine-stitched edge

Batting inside

10. With the machine-stitched side of the borders towards the quilt, whipstitch the borders to the quilt top by hand. Attach the borders to the sides first, then to the top and bottom edges of the quilt.

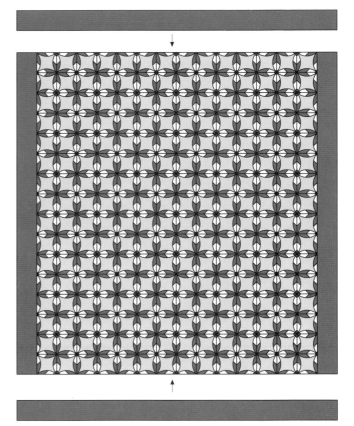

11. Finally, quilt the border. The Downside Quilters hand quilted a simple cable onto the borders.

Grazing the South Downs

BY SHARON CHAMBERS

*Grazing the South Downs by Sharon Chambers, 1994, Cowfold, England, 39" x 52½".
Hand and machine pieced and hand quilted.*

In addition to being famous for her outrageous earrings, Sharon is also well known for her animal quilts. She has made numerous quilts using different farmyard animals, and in Grazing the South Downs, she depicts a familiar scene of the English countryside.

Materials: 44"-wide fabric

1 yd. total assorted white, beige, tan, and black prints for bodies, ears, and tails

¼ yd. brown for legs

⅛ yd. total assorted brown and black prints for faces

1⅝ yds. green print (nondirectional) for background, sashing, borders, and binding

1⅝ yds. backing

Cutting

Use templates on the pullout pattern.

There are three different Sheep blocks in this quilt. Sheep Blocks A and B are the same size and can be interchanged to create a different flock. For variety, some of the A and B blocks have been reversed.

To make templates, trace the entire block design onto template plastic. Cut the pieces apart exactly on the drawn lines. Label each piece and the block type. Place the templates face down on the wrong side of the fabric and trace around the shape. For reversed pieces, place the templates face up on the wrong side of the fabric. Cut the shapes ¼" from the drawn line. Sew on the drawn lines. Follow the directions on page 66 if you prefer to quick-cut and sew the leg units; otherwise, you will need to cut individual pieces C and CX for the leg units.

Sheep Block A

Finished Block Size: 9" x 6"

LEFT-FACING SHEEP

From assorted sheep fabrics, cut:
    6 of Template A
From brown or black fabric, cut:
    6 of Template B
From green background, cut:
    6 of Template D
    6 of Template E
    6 of Template F
    6 of Template G

Brian Metz

Right-Facing Sheep

From sheep fabric, cut:
1 of Template A reversed
From brown or black fabric, cut:
1 of Template B reversed
From green background, cut:
1 of Template D reversed
1 of Template E reversed
1 of Template F reversed
1 of Template G reversed

Sheep Block B

Finished Block Size: 9" x 6"

Left-Facing Sheep

From assorted sheep fabric, cut:
5 of Template H
From brown or black fabric, cut:
5 of Template J
From green background fabric, cut:
5 and 5 reversed of Template F
5 of Template G
5 of Template K

Right-Facing Sheep

From assorted sheep fabric, cut:
3 of Template H reversed
From brown or black fabric, cut:
3 of Template J reversed
From green background fabric, cut:
3 and 3 reversed of Template F
3 of Template G reversed
3 of Template K reversed

Sheep Block C

Finished Block Size: 4½" x 6"

From assorted sheep fabric, cut:
2 of Template M
From green background fabric, cut:
2 and 2 reversed of Template F
2 and 2 reversed of Template G

Quick-Cut and -Piece Leg Units

*See steps 1 and 2 in the directions for
quick-piecing the leg units.*

From the brown fabric, cut:
4 strips, each 1" x 42"

From the green background fabric, cut:
2 strips, each 1" x 42"
1 strip, 2" x 42"

Note: If you prefer to cut and piece the leg units individually, cut the following pieces and assemble the leg units as shown below.

From brown fabric, cut:
64 of Template C
From green background fabric, cut:
32 of Template C
15 of Template CX

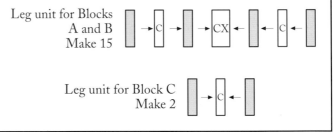

Leg unit for Blocks
A and B
Make 15

Leg unit for Block C
Make 2

Directions

1. To quick-piece the leg units, join the 1" brown strips, 1" and 2" background strips as shown to make a strip unit. Press the seam allowances towards the brown strips. Cut the strip unit into 16 segments, each 2" wide.

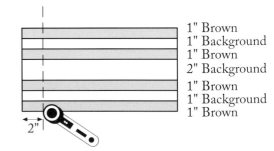

1" Brown
1" Background
1" Brown
2" Background
1" Brown
1" Background
1" Brown

2"

2. Remove the centre background piece in one of the leg units to make 2 single leg units for Block C.

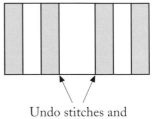

Undo stitches and
discard centre piece.

3. Using Templates N and O on page 69, make card-board or plastic templates for the ears and tails. Mark around the templates on the wrong side of the sheep fabric to match the sheep bodies. Pin 2 matching pieces of fabric together with right sides facing and the marked fabric on top. Sew on the pencil line around the shape, leaving the top edge open for turning.

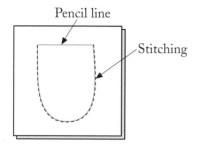

Pencil line

Stitching

4. Cut out the shape, leaving a ¼"-wide seam allowance at the open edge for turning and trimming the rest of the seam allowance to ³⁄₁₆".

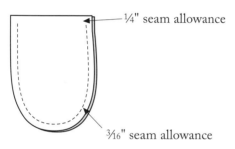

¼" seam allowance

³⁄₁₆" seam allowance

5. Turn the ears and tail right sides out and finger-press. Stuff the ears and tail with a wisp of batting if you desire. Baste the ears in place on the body of the sheep as indicated on the template diagram. The raw edges will be caught in the seam allowance when the block is stitched. For the tails, turn the raw edges of the opening to the inside of the tail and appliqué the top edge on the sheep body so that it hangs free.

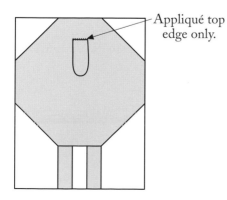

Appliqué top edge only.

6. Lay out the pieces for each block before you start to sew. Following the piecing diagrams, join the pieces. See the Tip Box on page 68 for pointers on sewing set-in seams.

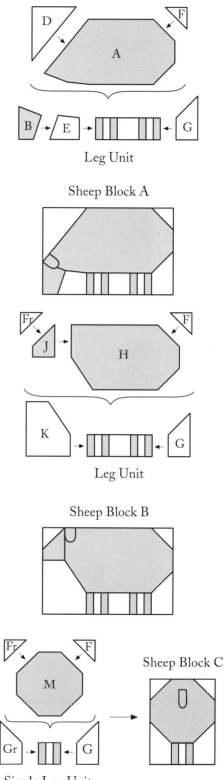

Leg Unit

Sheep Block A

Leg Unit

Sheep Block B

Sheep Block C

Single Leg Unit

Tip

When you join the bottom half of the block to the top half, you will need to sew the seam in three separate steps. The pieces must be joined so that they can be pivoted as they are set into each other. The following procedure will allow you to set in the seams with very little trouble and give you a very neat join.

When you sew a piece to a leg unit, begin stitching ¼" from the inside edge and continue to the bottom edge as shown. Do this for each piece that is joined to a leg unit.

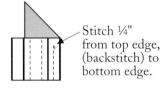

Stitch ¼" from top edge, (backstitch) to bottom edge.

With right sides together, pin the bottom of the sheep body to the top of the leg unit, aligning the raw edges of both pieces. Sew from seam line to seam line.

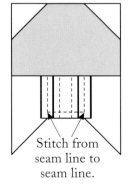

Stitch from seam line to seam line.

To sew the sides, pivot one of the pieces next to the leg unit so that the raw edges are even with the sheep body; pin generously. Be careful not to stretch the pieces. Sew from the seam line to the outside edge. Repeat with the other side of the leg unit. Press the seam allowances towards the sheep body.

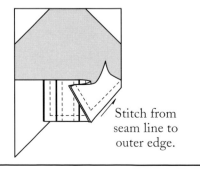

Stitch from seam line to outer edge.

Assembling the Blocks

1. Refer to the diagram below for help in identifying the position of the blocks, sashing strips, and borders. Label the pieces after you cut them to avoid confusion.

From the background fabric, cut:

6 strips, each 2" x 42". From each of 5 strips, cut 1 strip, 2" x 30½" (J), and 1 strip, 2" x 6½" (D). From the remaining strip, cut 1 strip, 2" x 6½" (D), and 2 strips, each 2" x 9½" (F).

1 strip, 6½" x 42"; crosscut into 6 squares, each 6½" x 6½" (E).

2 strips, each 5" x 42"; from each strip, cut 1 strip, 5" x 21½" (H), and 1 strip, 5" x 20" (K).

2 strips, each 5" x 42"; from each strip, cut 1 strip, 5" x 27½" (L), and 1 strip, 3½" x 9½" (G).

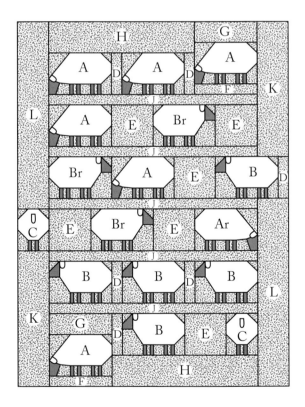

2. Following the piecing diagram, sew the blocks, sashing strips, and border strips together. Press the seam allowances towards the sheep bodies; this enhances the three-dimensional effect.

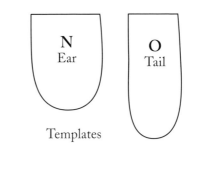

Templates

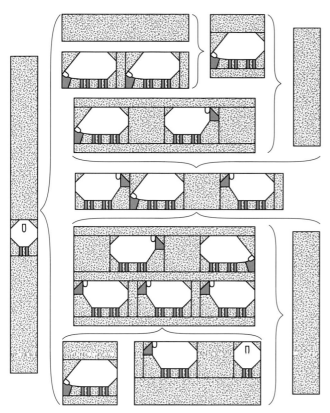

3. Layer the quilt with batting and backing; baste. Quilt in-the-ditch around each sheep; add other quilting as desired. Bind the edges.
4. Sign and date your quilt.

Summer Pudding

8 to 10 slices of day-old white bread
1½ to 2 lbs. mixed summer fruits
(red, white, and black currants; raspberries;
strawberries; and pitted red cherries)
½ to ¾ cup granulated sugar

Trim the crusts off the bread. Cut a circle from 1 slice of bread to fit the bottom of a 1½-pint pudding bowl. Arrange slices to line the sides of the bowl, cutting them if necessary, making sure there are no gaps. Reserve some bread to cover the top. Wash and prepare the fruit and put it in a saucepan with the sugar. Cover the pan and cook for 5 minutes or until the fruit is soft. Pour hot fruit into the lined bowl. Cover the top of the fruit with the remaining bread and put a small plate on top. Press down lightly on the bread and place a 2-lb. weight on the plate. Refrigerate overnight. Invert the pudding onto a serving dish and serve with cream. Serves 6.

Friendship Triangles

BY PAT KEATING

Friendship Triangles by Pat Keating, 1993, Redhill, England, 54½" x 69½". Machine pieced and quilted.

Pat's quilt is made from 600 triangles, each from a different fabric—and she can remember from where and whom all the fabrics came. Each block is made up of 50 triangles.

Materials: 44"-wide fabric

1⅞ yds. total light scraps

1⅞ yds. total dark scraps

½ yd. inner border

¾ yd. outer border

½ yd. binding

3½ yds. backing

Cutting

Cut strips across the width of the fabric.
All measurements include ¼"-wide seam allowances.

From the light fabric scraps, cut:
    156 squares, each 3⅞" x 3⅞"; cut squares once
        diagonally to yield 312 half-square triangles
From the dark fabric scraps, cut:
    144 squares, each 3⅞" x 3⅞"; cut squares once
        diagonally to yield 288 half-square triangles

Note: Cutting the triangles in the above manner will re-
    sult in 2 triangles from the same fabric. If you want
    all the triangles to be from different fabrics, cut indi-
    vidual triangles using the template on the pullout
    pattern.

From the inner border fabric, cut:
    5 strips, each 2½" x 42"
From the outer border fabric, cut:
    6 strips, each 4" x 42"
From the binding fabric, cut:
    6 strips, each 2½" x 42"

Directions

1. Following the block diagram below, arrange the light and dark triangles. It's very important to have good contrast between the light and dark triangles to create the octagon in the middle of the block; the squares are created when the blocks are sewn together.

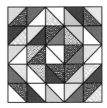

2. Join the half-square triangles to make pieced squares. Join the pieced squares in horizontal rows; press the seams in opposite directions from row to row. Join the rows to complete the block. Make 12 blocks.
3. Arrange the blocks in 4 rows of 3 blocks each. Join the blocks in horizontal rows; press the seams in opposite directions from row to row. Join the rows.

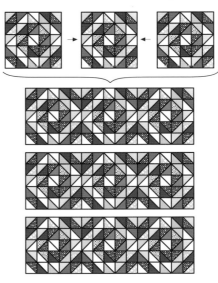

4. Following directions on pages 83– 84 for straight-cut borders, measure, cut, and sew the 2½"-wide inner border strips to the quilt. Repeat with the 4"-wide outer border strips.
5. Layer the quilt with batting and backing; baste. Quilt as desired and bind the edges.
6. Sign and date your quilt.

Black Gold

BY SHARON CHAMBERS

Black Gold by Sharon Chambers, 1994, Cowfold, England, 34" x 34". Hand and machine pieced and hand quilted.

Cutting

Cut strips across the width of the fabric.
All measurements include ¼"-wide seam allowances.
Use the templates on the pullout pattern.

From the assorted yellow and gold fabrics, cut:
    a total of 16 of Template A
    a total of 12 of Template B
    a total of 2 of Template C

From the black directional print, cut:
    11 of Template A
    7 of Template B

From the assorted black fabrics, cut:
    a total of 9 of Template A
    a total of 17 of Template B
    a total of 7 of Template C

From the rust fabric, cut:
    4 strips, each 1¼" x 42", for inner border

From the black fabric, cut:
    4 strips, each 3¼" x 42", for outer border

From the binding fabric, cut:
    4 strips, each 2½" x 42"

Sharon introduces the World without End block to her students quite early in her beginners' course. This beautiful wall hanging shows just what can be done with a simple block and a bit of imagination. Sharon has continued her design into the border for added interest; however, the instructions given here are for plain borders.

Materials: 44"-wide fabric

¾ yd. total assorted yellows and golds

½ yd. black directional print

1 yd. total assorted blacks

¼ yd. rust for inner border

½ yd. black for outer border

⅜ yd. binding

1 yd. backing

Directions

1. Arrange the various colours of the A, B, and C pieces, following the diagram below or in a design of your own.

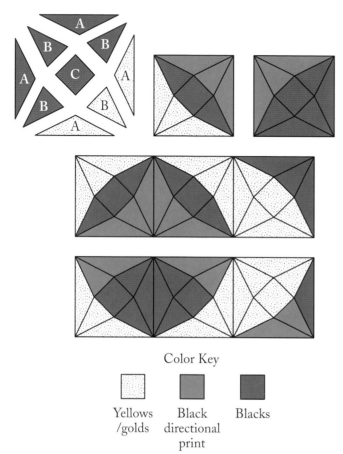

Color Key

Yellows /golds | Black directional print | Blacks

2. Join the pieces for each block as shown in the piecing diagram. Press the seams towards the B pieces. When sewing A to B, stitch from the outside corner to within ¼" of the inside corner; backstitch. When sewing B to C, stitch from edge to edge.

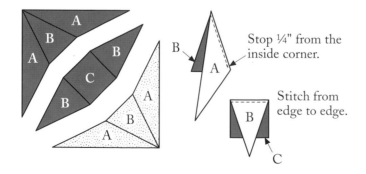

Stop ¼" from the inside corner.

Stitch from edge to edge.

3. To sew the A/B/A units to the B/C/B units, match the B and C pieces together and sew the centre seam from seam line to seam line.

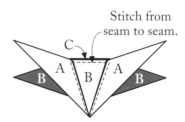

Stitch from seam to seam.

4. To finish sewing the units together, twist piece A slightly so that the raw edge of piece A and piece B are even. Be careful not to pull the pieces out of shape. Sew the seam from the centre to the outer edge. Repeat with the other side. Press the seams towards the B/C/B unit.

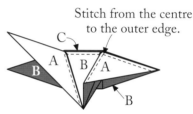

Stitch from the centre to the outer edge.

5. Join the blocks in horizontal rows. Press the seams in opposite directions from row to row. Join the rows.

6. Join a rust border strip to a black border strip to make a single border unit. Make 4. Following directions on page 84 for borders with mitred corners, measure, cut, and sew the border strips to the quilt.

Rust
Black

Make 4

7. Layer the quilt with batting and backing; baste. Quilt as desired and bind the edges.

8. Sign and date your quilt.

Sunset Flight

BY PAM ANSTEY

Sunset Flight by Pam Anstey, 1994, Horsted Keynes, England, 32" x 40". Machine pieced and quilted.

> This quilt depicts birds flying home to roost over the lakes, behind Pam's cottage. She always has such wonderful sunsets.

Materials: 44"-wide fabric

1⅛ yds. black (includes border and binding)

¾ yd. total assorted reds

¼ yd. total assorted purples

¼ yd. total assorted yellows

¼ yd. total assorted blues

⅜ yd. total assorted greens

1 yd. backing

Cutting

Cut strips across the width of the fabric.
All measurements include ¼"-wide seam allowances.

From the black fabric, cut:
   7 strips, each 2⅞" x 42"; crosscut into 91 squares,
      each 2⅞" x 2⅞"; cut squares once diagonally to
      yield 182 half-square triangles
   3 strips, each 2½" x 42", for borders
   3 strips, each 2½" x 42", for binding

From the assorted fabrics, cut strips 2⅞" wide.

The number of strips you need to cut depends on how many assorted fabrics you are using and how many triangles of each colour you want to use. For our quilt, we cut the following number of squares and half-square triangles.

Fabric	No. of Squares	No. of Triangles
Reds	97	194
Purples	24	48
Yellows	20	40
Blues	19	38
Greens	30	60

From one of the red fabrics, cut:
   1 strip, 2½" x 42", for binding
From one of the green fabrics, cut:
   1 strip, 2½" x 42", for binding

Directions

1. Following the diagram below, arrange the half-square triangles. Join the half-square triangles to make pieced squares. Press the seams towards the darker fabric.
2. Join the pieced squares in horizontal rows, omitting the pieced squares in the outer border for now. Press the seams in opposite directions from row to row.
3. Join the rows together to complete the centre of the quilt. Press the seams in one direction.
4. Trim 3 of the 2½" black strips to the following lengths:
      2½" x 22½" for left border strip
      2½" x 34½" for right border strip
      2½" x 20½" for bottom border strip

London Omnibus

Note: It's a good idea to double-check the measurements of the border strips for your quilt, just in case the centre of your quilt is a slightly different size. Remember to add ½" to your measurements for seam allowances.

5. Join the pieced squares to the black border strips. Sew the side border strips to the quilt before adding the bottom border strip.

6. Layer the quilt with batting and backing; baste. Quilt as desired. Bind the edges using the 2½" wide black, red, and green strips.

7. Sign and date your quilt.

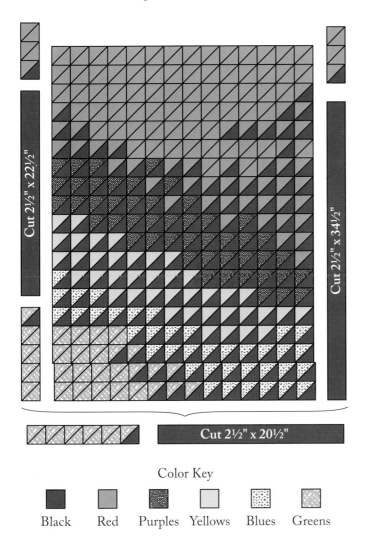

Cut 2½" x 22½"

Cut 2½" x 34½"

Cut 2½" x 20½"

Color Key

Black   Red   Purples   Yellows   Blues   Greens

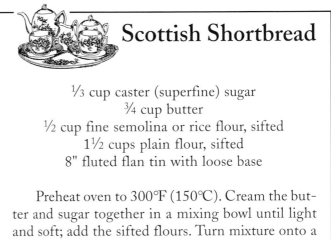

Scottish Shortbread

⅓ cup caster (superfine) sugar
¾ cup butter
½ cup fine semolina or rice flour, sifted
1½ cups plain flour, sifted
8" fluted flan tin with loose base

Preheat oven to 300°F (150°C). Cream the butter and sugar together in a mixing bowl until light and soft; add the sifted flours. Turn mixture onto a pastry board and work with your fingertips until you have a smooth dough. Roll it out until it is roughly the size of your tin; press evenly into the tin. Prick shortbread all over with a fork. Bake for about 1 hour on the centre shelf. Remove from oven. Using a palette knife, mark the surface into 12 wedges while it's still warm. Leave to cool in the tin; then cut into the 12 portions and store in an airtight tin. In summer, try spreading the round of shortbread with whipped cream and top with strawberries just before serving. Serves 12.

Basic Techniques

EQUIPMENT AND SUPPLIES

Sewing Machine: You need a sewing machine in good working order for machine piecing.

Scissors: Use your best scissors to cut fabric only. Use an older pair for cutting cardboard and template plastic.

Rotary-Cutting Equipment: You will need a rotary cutter, cutting mat, and clear acrylic cutting rulers. Two handy sizes include a 6" x 24" ruler and a 6" square. The ScrapMaster is a very handy ruler for cutting triangles and squares from scraps.

Thread: Use good-quality, all-purpose cotton thread for piecing. Select a light neutral colour for light-coloured fabrics, and a dark neutral colour for dark-coloured fabrics. Thread for appliqué should match the colour of the appliqué pieces, not the background fabric. Use quilting thread only for quilting. It is thicker than regular thread and may show if used for piecing or appliqué.

Needles: For machine piecing, a fine needle (10/70) works well for most cottons. Use size 12/80 for heavier fabrics. For hand piecing, a thin needle (sizes 8–12) will slide through the fabrics easily as you piece. Select a needle that is comfortable for you to use and easy to thread.

Pins: Long quilters' pins with glass or plastic heads are easy to handle.

Template Plastic: Use clear or frosted plastic to make durable, accurate templates. This plastic is available at most quilt shops.

Seam Ripper: Use this tool to remove stitches from incorrectly sewn seams.

Marking Tools: You can mark quilting lines or draw around templates on most fabrics with a regular pencil or a mechanical pencil. Use a silver or yellow marking pencil on darker fabrics. Chalk pencils or chalk-wheel markers also make clear marks on fabric. A Hera marker is a plastic tool that creases the fabric. The crease is very easy to see. No matter what tool you decide to use, be sure to test it on your fabrics to make certain you can remove the marks without damaging your fabric.

ROTARY CUTTING

Many of the quilts in this book are rotary cut. The rotary cutter speeds up the cutting process so that, coupled with machine piecing, patchwork quilts really can be made accurately and efficiently in a fraction of the time it takes to hand piece them. And if you love hand sewing, why not put all your efforts into hand quilting? Most of our quick quilts are machine quilted for speed, but there is nothing to compare with a lovingly hand-quilted piece of work.

1. To straighten the edge of the fabric, fold the fabric in half, selvage to selvage, then fold again, aligning the folded edge with the selvages. Place the ruler across the fabric so that one of the perpendicular lines is aligned with the double fold of the fabric. Hold the ruler firmly with your left hand and the cutter in the right. Keeping the blade against the edge of the ruler, push the cutter away from your body in one even movement.

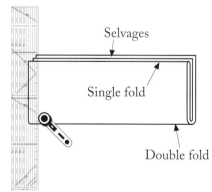

Selvages

Single fold

Double fold

Note: Left-handed people should reverse these instructions, but the important thing is always to cut away from the body.

2. To cut strips, align the desired measurement on the ruler with the clean-cut edge of the fabric. Hold the ruler firmly with your left hand and cut strips, moving from left to right across the fabric. Every 4 to 6 cuts, check to make sure that the fabric is still straight by opening up a strip.

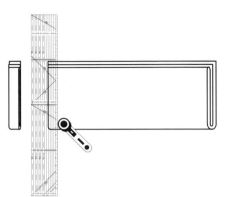

Note: If the cuts are not perpendicular to the fold, the strips will form a shallow zigzag when opened, and you will need to repeat step 1 to restraighten the edge.

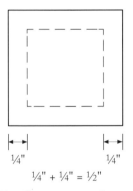

Cutting Squares and Rectangles

1. Cut a strip the finished width of the square or rectangle plus ½" for seam allowances.

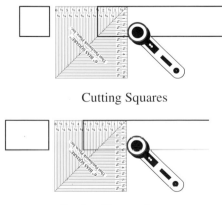

¼"   ¼"

¼" + ¼" = ½"

2. Using the Bias Square, cut the strips into squares or rectangles, remembering to add the seam allowance.

Cutting Squares

Cutting Rectangles

PIECED SQUARES

There are various methods of speeding up the piecing of half-square triangle units, but for most of the quilts in this book, where we use lots of scraps to make half-square triangles, we simply cut the correct size square, cut it once diagonally, stack the triangles, and then nub the points. Then two triangles are stitched to make a pieced square.

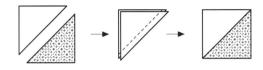

Cutting Half-Square Triangles

Half-square triangles are cut from a square so that the two shorter sides are on the straight of grain, and the long side is on the bias. To determine the size square to cut, add ⅞" to the finished short side of the triangle. For example, if the finished short side of the triangle is 4", cut a square measuring 4⅞"; then cut the square once diagonally to yield two half-square triangles.

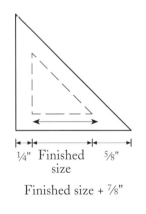

¼"   Finished   ⅝"
       size

Finished size + ⅞"

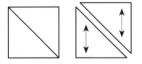

Nubbing Half-Square Triangles

Add ½" to the finished dimension of the triangle's short side and place the Bias Square ruler on the triangle at this mark. Cut off the points. For example, to nub a 4" (finished size) half-square triangle, place the Bias Square on the 4½" mark as shown and trim.

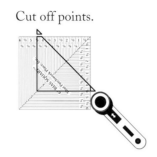

Cut off points.

Cutting Quarter-Square Triangles

Quarter-square triangles are cut from squares so that their short sides are on the bias and the long side is on the straight of grain. To determine the size square to cut, add 1¼" to the finished size of the long side of the triangle. For example, if the finished size of the long side of the triangle is 4", cut a square 5¼"; then cut the square twice diagonally to yield four quarter-square triangles.

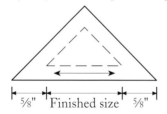

⅝" | Finished size | ⅝"

Finished size + 1¼"

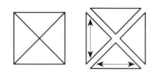

Nubbing Quarter-Square Triangles

To nub quarter-square triangles, you will have to make two separate cuts.

1. For the first cut, add ⅞" to the finished size of the triangle's long edge and measure this distance from the left corner towards the right. Cut the excess fabric to the right of the Bias Square edge.

2. For the second cut, add ½" to the finished size of the triangle's long edge, turn the triangle over, and measure this distance from the first nub to the right. Cut the excess fabric to the right of the Bias Square edge. For example, to nub a 4" (finished size) quarter-square triangle, nub first at 4⅞" (4" + ⅞") and second at 4½" (4" + ½").

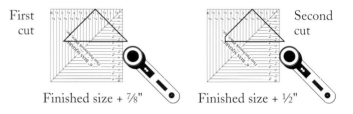

First cut — Finished size + ⅞"   Second cut — Finished size + ½"

MACHINE PIECING

In all patchwork, the finished effect depends on the degree of care and accuracy used in all stages of construction. Accuracy is achieved by using a consistent ¼"-wide seam allowance throughout. For machine piecing, a scant ¼"-wide seam allowance is preferable. Before starting to sew, check the distance between the needle and the right-hand edge of the presser foot. The needle on many sewing machines can be adjusted to obtain a scant ¼". If your machine does not have this feature, you can make a guide by applying a piece of masking tape on the throat plate a scant ¼" from the needle.

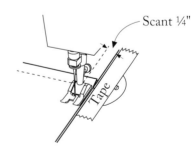

Scant ¼"

Tape

1. With right sides together, align the raw edges and pin.
2. Using a stitch length of 12 stitches per inch, stitch the pieces together from raw edge to raw edge.

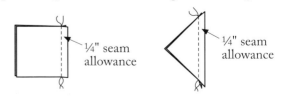

¼" seam allowance   ¼" seam allowance

CHAIN PIECING

Chain piecing is the technique of feeding pieces through the sewing machine without lifting the presser foot and without cutting the thread. Always chain piece when you can—it saves time and thread.

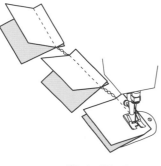

Chain Piecing

HAND PIECING

Hand piecing is a very relaxing process for many quilters. Because it makes the work portable, it also allows them to work on projects in spare moments. Just as in machine piecing, maintaining a ¼"-wide seam allowance is very important.

1. When making templates for hand piecing, do not include seam allowances. Trace templates onto cardboard or template plastic, tracing on the dashed seam line instead of the cutting line.
2. Place the template face down on the wrong side of the fabric, aligning the grain-line arrow with the straight grain of the fabric. Use a sharp pencil to trace around the template. The marked line is the stitching line. If you need several of the same template, leave at least ½" between the marked pieces for seam allowances.
3. Add a ¼"-wide seam allowance all around each traced shape. Use a ruler and a sharp pencil. Cut out the template on the outer line. Some quilters merely "eyeball" the ¼" seam allowance while cutting, since they will be matching the drawn stitching lines when joining pieces. Do whichever is most comfortable and accurate for you.
4. Matching the drawn seam lines, place two pieces together with right sides facing; pin.
5. Starting with a small backstitch on one end of the drawn line and using a small running stitch, sew directly on the line. Do not stitch into the seam allow-

ances. Check to make sure you are stitching on the lines of both pieces. Continue stitching on the line to the opposite end of the drawn line; backstitch over the last stitch. When seams within a block intersect each other, take a small backstitch on each side of the seam-allowance intersection to hold it securely; do not tack the seam allowance down.

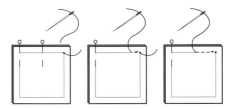

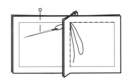

PRESSING

Pressing is of paramount importance at every stage.
1. Always try to press pairs of squares or triangles so that one set of seam allowances goes one way and the other set goes the opposite way. This creates less bulk.

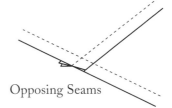

Opposing Seams

2. Press seams towards the darker fabric wherever possible.
3. When pressing a set of strips, place strips across the ironing board, wrong side up, with the darker strip on the left. Holding the fabric with the left hand, iron from the right, pressing the seams towards the left. Turn the strips over and press on the right side of the fabric in the same manner. This will prevent folds in the seams.

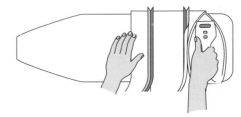

APPLIQUÉ TECHNIQUES

Freezer-Paper Appliqué

Use freezer paper to make perfectly shaped appliqués.

1. Place the freezer paper, plastic-coated side down, on top of the pattern and trace the design with a pencil. Cut out the freezer-paper design exactly on the pencil line. *Do not add seam allowances.*

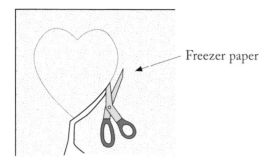

Freezer paper

2. With the plastic-coated side of the freezer paper on the wrong side of the fabric, iron the freezer paper in place with a hot, dry iron. Cut out the shape, adding a ¼"-wide seam allowance all around.

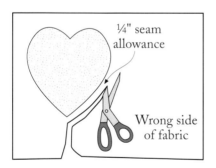

¼" seam allowance

Wrong side of fabric

3. Turn and baste the seam allowance over the freezer-paper edges by hand or use a glue stick.

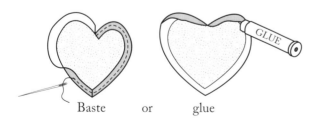

Baste　　or　　glue

4. Pin the design in place to the background fabric and appliqué, using the traditional appliqué stitch (on page 83).

5. After the design has been appliquéd, remove any basting stitches. Carefully cut a small slit in the background fabric behind the appliqué and remove the freezer paper with tweezers. Cut away background fabric leaving a ¼"-wide seam allowance. If you used a glue stick, soak the piece in warm water for a few minutes to release the glue before removing the paper.

Cut away background fabric only.

Leave ¼" seam allowance all around.

Needle-Turn Appliqué

With this method, you do not need a paper template and you do not need to turn under and baste the seam allowances prior to appliqué.

1. Using a plastic or cardboard template, trace the design onto the right side of the fabric. Cut out the design ⅛" to ³⁄₁₆" from the drawn line.

2. Pin or baste the design onto the background fabric. Starting on a straight edge, turn the seam allowance under with the tip of the needle and hold it in place with your thumb. Stitch the appliqué, using the traditional appliqué stitch (on page 83). Turn under only small portions of the seam allowance at a time as you stitch.

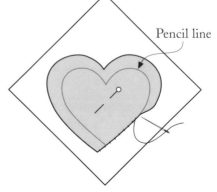

Pencil line

Traditional Appliqué Stitch

The blind stitch or appliqué stitch is appropriate for sewing all appliqué shapes.

1. Tie a knot in a single strand of thread approximately 18" long.
2. Hide the knot by slipping the needle into the seam allowance from the wrong side of the appliqué, bringing it out on the fold line.
3. Start the first stitch by moving the needle straight off the appliqué and inserting the needle into the background. Let the needle travel under the background fabric, parallel to the edge of the appliqué, bringing it up about ⅛" away.
4. As you bring the needle up, pierce the edge of the appliqué, catching only one or two threads of the folded edge.
5. Move the needle straight off the appliqué into the background fabric and bring it up about ⅛" away, again travelling under the background fabric and catching only the edge of the appliqué.
6. Give the thread a slight tug and continue stitching.

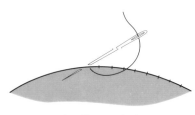

Appliqué stitch

7. To end your stitches, pull the needle through to the back side. Take two small stitches behind the appliqué and cut the thread. Make sure the tail of your thread does not shadow through the background. If it does, take one more small stitch through the back side of the appliqué to direct the tail of the thread under the appliqué fabric.

BORDERS

Borders are extremely useful in that they can extend your quilt to the exact size required, or they can frame the design effectively. They do, however, need to be in proportion to the quilt. If a very wide border is required, it is better to have two or three borders of varying widths rather than just one. Borders can be intricately pieced, made from solid fabric and elaborately quilted, or made from border print fabric. The corners can be either straight or mitred.

Fabric requirements for the borders in this book are based on cutting strips across the width of the fabric, a method that is usually more economical. The strips are then joined to the required length. If you don't want seams in the border strips, you can cut the strips on the lengthwise grain of the fabric. This will, however, require extra yardage to obtain the required lengths, but you will have fabric left over to add to your collection.

Borders with Straight-Cut Corners

1. Measure the length of the quilt through the centre and cut two border strips to this length. Piece as necessary to obtain the required length. Mark the halves and quarters of the quilt edges and the border strips with pins. Pin the border strips to the sides of the quilt, matching the pins and ends and easing where necessary. Stitch and press the seam allowances towards the border.

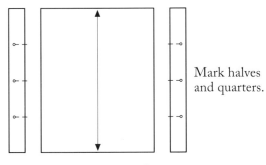

Mark halves and quarters.

Measure centre of quilt, top to bottom.

2. Measure the width of the quilt through the centre, including the borders just added. Cut two border strips to that measurement. Piece as necessary to obtain the required length. Mark the halves and quarters of the border edges and quilt edges. Pin the borders to the top and bottom edges of the quilt, matching the pins and ends and easing where necessary. Stitch and press the seam allowances towards the border.

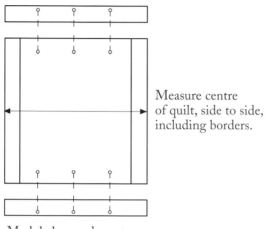

Measure centre of quilt, side to side, including borders.

Mark halves and quarters.

Borders with Mitred Corners

1. Measure the length of the quilt through the centre as above, but cut two border strips the length of the quilt plus twice the width of the border. In the same manner, measure and cut two strips the width of the quilt, also adding twice the width of the border.

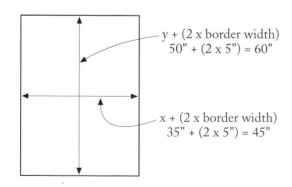

y + (2 x border width)
50" + (2 x 5") = 60"

x + (2 x border width)
35" + (2 x 5") = 45"

2. Mark the halves and quarters of the quilt edges and the border strips. Matching the pins, begin stitching ¼" from the corner of the quilt and continue to the other end, stopping ¼" from the corner of the quilt. Backstitch at both ends. Leave the width of the border hanging free at both ends. Repeat with all four border strips.

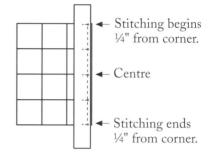

← Stitching begins ¼" from corner.

← Centre

← Stitching ends ¼" from corner.

3. Place the quilt right side up on your ironing board. Fold one border strip under itself at a 45° angle. Press and slipstitch in place; trim the excess fabric. Repeat with remaining corners.

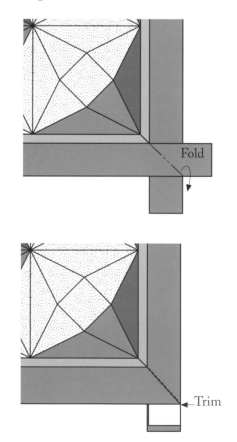

Fold

Trim

MARKING THE QUILTING LINES

Whether or not to mark the quilt designs depends on the type of quilting you will be doing. Marking is not necessary if you will be quilting in-the-ditch or outline quilting a uniform distance from the seam lines. More complex designs will need to be marked on the quilt top before layering with batting and backing. Choose a tool that will be visible on your fabric and test it to make sure that the marks can be easily removed.

LAYERING THE QUILT

Batting (Wadding)

Batting comes packaged in standard bed sizes, or it can be purchased by the yard. In England, a 2-ounce polyester wadding is recommended for hand quilting. This is roughly equivalent to the low-loft batting available in the United States. For a flatter finish, thinner batting is also available in 100% cotton, 100% polyester, or a combination of the two. If using 100% cotton, you must quilt very densely (every 2" to 3") or it will shift. Use thick battings only when you plan to tie a quilt. Cut the batting at least 3" larger than the quilt top all the way around.

Backing

The backing should be at least 3" larger than the quilt top. For large quilts, it is usually necessary to join two or three lengths of fabric to make a backing of the required size. Press the seams open to make quilting easier.

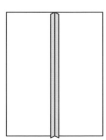

Two Lengths of Fabric
Seamed in the Centre

1 fabric width

Partial Fabric Width

Basting the Layers

1. Cut the backing and batting at least 3" larger than your quilt top all the way around.
2. Lay the backing fabric right side down on a smooth surface. Tape the corners to hold the fabric down flat. Lay the batting on top, taking care to smooth out any wrinkles. Lay the quilt top, right side up, on top. Baste the three layers together in a grid, starting in the centre and working out to the edges. The rows of basting should be about 6" apart. Or, if machine quilting, you can pin-baste the three layers together with 1" safety pins, again every 6". Avoid placing the pins on quilting lines.

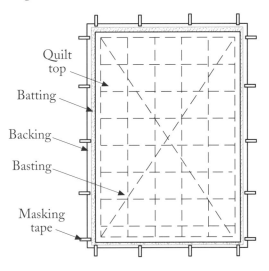

Quilt top

Batting

Backing

Basting

Masking tape

QUILTING

To hand quilt or machine quilt? At one time, machine quilting was seen as a very inferior option, but not so nowadays, with techniques improving all the time. We normally end up machine quilting simply through lack of time, but both of us still love the softer look of hand quilting. The choice is yours—there is a place for both techniques.

BINDING

A double-fold French binding gives a professional finish, whether you are using straight or bias binding. If your quilt has curved edges, you must use bias binding, but if your quilt has straight sides, you can use either straight or bias binding.

To cut straight-grain strips:

Cut 2½"-wide strips across the width of the fabric. Cut enough strips to go around the perimeter of your quilt plus approximately 10" for the corners and for overlapping the ends. Sew the strips together, end to end, to make one long piece of binding. Press the seam allowances open.

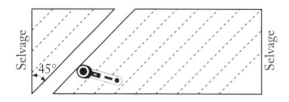

Joining Straight-Cut Strips

To cut bias-grain strips:

1. Using the 45°-angle line on a long cutting ruler as a guide, make a bias cut across one corner of a length of fabric. Cut 2½"-wide strips parallel to the first cut across the length of the fabric.

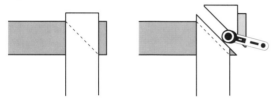

2. Seam the ends to make one long piece of binding. Press the seam allowances open.

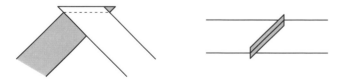

To attach the binding to the quilt:

1. Trim the excess backing and batting so that they extend ¼" beyond the edge of the quilt top.

2. At one end of the binding strip, turn under ¼" at a 45° angle and press. Then fold the binding in half lengthwise, wrong sides together, and press.

Fold line

3. Starting about 12" from one corner, align the edges of the binding with the edge of the quilt top (not the extended batting and backing) and pin. Stitch, using a ¼"-wide seam allowance. At the first corner, stop ¼" from the edge of the quilt top and backstitch.

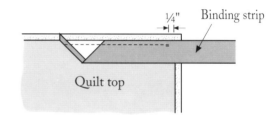

¼"   Binding strip

Quilt top

4. Fold the binding up, away from the quilt, then back down onto itself, making sure the edge of the binding is parallel to the edge of the quilt top. Begin stitching at the edge, backstitching to secure the corner stitches. Repeat with remaining edges and corners of the quilt.

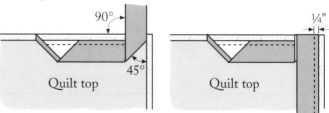

90°

Quilt top

45°

¼"

Quilt top

5. When you come to the starting point, overlap the beginning stitches by about 1" and trim the end at a 45° angle.

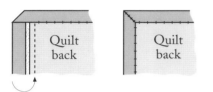

Quilt top

6. To create a neat mitre on the reverse of the quilt, fold over the binding to the back of the quilt so that it covers the stitching line. Blindstitch in place.

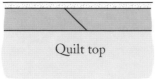

Quilt back   Quilt back

Signing Your Quilt

It is important that all quilts, however small, are signed and dated either on the front, making a feature of it, or on the back. Also, why not put some interesting details about the quilt, why it was made, its title, who it was made for and how long it took? We all know how interested we are when finding details like this about old quilts—let's give the quilters of the future an easier time in their research.

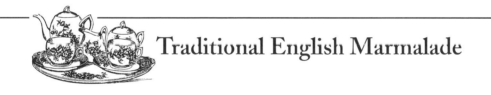

Traditional English Marmalade

3 lbs. Seville (bitter) oranges
9 cups water
12 cups granulated sugar
juice of 2 lemons

Scrub the oranges. Put whole oranges into a large saucepan with 8 cups (2 quarts) of the water. Cover with a lid and simmer for about 2 hours or until the fruit is soft. (Test with a knife.)

Using a slottted spoon, transfer oranges to a bowl; reserve the liquid. When the oranges are cool enough to handle, cut fruit in half and scoop out the pith and pulp with the pips and put into a separate saucepan. Add the remaining 1 cup water and simmer for 10 minutes. Meanwhile, coarsely chop the orange peel. A blender or mincer can be used for a finer texture.

Add the cut peel to the reserved cooking liquid. Strain the liquid from the pith and pips into the pan and add the sugar and lemon juice. Stir over low heat until the sugar has dissolved. Bring to a boil and boil rapidly for about 15 minutes. Draw off the heat and test for a set. Skim the surface. Allow to cool for 15 to 20 minutes; then stir once and pour into warmed, dry jars. Cover and seal. Makes 8 pounds.

That Patchwork Place Publications and Products